FOR SIMON

For Simon. A Journey into Truth and Reconciliation is a continuation of the narrative in *Death in the Delta: Uncovering a Mississippi Family Secret*. New evidence emerges and unites two families torn by tragedy.

—FOR—
SIMON

A Journey into Truth and Reconciliation

MOLLY WALLING

LUMINARE PRESS

WWW.LUMINAREPRESS.COM

Printed in the United States of America

Cover Design by Melissa K. Thomas

Luminare Press
442 Charnelton St.
Eugene, OR 97401
www.luminarepress.com

LCCN: 2020910170
ISBN: 978-1-64388-360-1

for Whitney and Kate

Contents

Cast of Characters

MY FAMILY—THE FIELDS

Harris Jesse and Martha Catherine
(great grandparents)

Thomas and Rebekah
(grandparents)

Jay

Tom

Bill

Sis

THE TOOMBS

Leana and Shelby
(Simon's parents)

Simon

Virginia
(Simon's only child)

Pat

Latoya

Gregory

ANOTHER CONNECTION

Mattie Wingate
(aka "Aunt Mat" and "Otta")
Cook on the Fields plantation

Charlie Lee Anderson, Jr.
(Mat's grandson), (Virginia's husband)

TIMELINE

Fields Family	U.S./World Events	Toombs Family
1842 Jesse Rawls Fields moves from NC to MS		
	1849 California Gold Rush	
	1861-1865 Civil War	
	1863 Emancipation Proclamation	
1866 Harris Jesse Fields Martha Catherine Sullivan wed		
1882 Thomas Walter Fields born		
		1876 Mattie Sturdivant Winegate born
	1877 Reconstruction	
	1896 Plessy v. Ferguson	
1901 Rebekah Blanks Fields born		
		1911 Simon Toombs born
	1914-1918 World War I Start of Great Migration	

Fields Family	U.S./World Events	Toombs Family
1920 H.J. gives Ashland Plantation to Thomas		
1921 Thomas marries Rebekah		
1922 H.J. Fields—"Jay" (my father) born		
1924 Tom Fields born		
1926 Bill Fields born		
	1927 Great Flood of Mississippi River	
1929 Frances (Sis) Fields born	1929 Wall Street Crash	
		1930 Charlie Lee Anderson born
1931 Fields family moves to Greenfields		
		1932 Virginia Toombs born
1935 Thomas Fields dies		
	1937 Great Depression	

Fields Family	U.S./World Events	Toombs Family
	1939-1945 World War II	
		1941 Simon enlists
1943 Jay enlists		
		1944 Charlie Lee's father to CA
1945 Jay marries Betsy Fleming		
	Dec. 12, 1946 Simon shot and killed by Fields brothers	
1947 Jay goes before grand jury		
		1948 Charlie Lee & Virginia move to CA

PREFACE

I refuse to accept the view that mankind is so tragically bound to the starless midnight of racism and war that the bright daybreak of peace and brotherhood can never become a reality...I believe that unarmed truth and unconditional love will have the final word.

MARTIN LUTHER KING, JR.

For Simon follows the African American family of Simon Toombs, the man I introduced to the reading public in my 2012 book, *Death in the Delta: Uncovering a Mississippi Family Secret.* For sixty years my family managed to sequester a story of racial violence that had ended in the death of two black men. At the close of WWII my father, H. J. Fields returned from service in the army air corp to the family plantation in the Mississippi Delta. He and his brothers drove into town on the night of December 12, 1946, determined to shut down the juke jive where black farm workers were gathering to drink and socialize. After the Fields men met with resistance, a fight broke out and two black men, Simon Toombs and David Jones, lay dead from gunshot wounds. My father was charged with manslaughter, but an all-white grand jury did not find cause to continue to trial.

My family framed an allegation of self-defense and did not speak of that disastrous day. The social climate established by Jim Crow legislation colluded in the cover-up. Though the story was carried in three newspapers in Mississippi, it was not widely known. The incident attested to the deeply degraded position of blacks, their lack of defenses and legal protections in the culture of the Deep South.

At the time I wrote the original story, I believed Simon was childless when he died. Even his army records stated, "no dependents," but soon after *Death in the Delta* was published in 2012, I was contacted by Simon's great-great-grandson, who confirmed that Simon had a daughter, Virginia Toombs Anderson, who was alive and well in California. Her husband, Charles Lee Anderson, was raised by his grandmother, Mattie Wingate, the cook at my family's plantation home in the Delta. Charlie Lee grew up knowing my father and his family intimately.

After publication and a brief book tour, depression began to settle in me. I felt bereft after working on my project for nearly nine years. The void was so deep and wide it felt as if I'd lost a dear friend. So many unresolved questions raised by *Death in the Delta* left me feeling no real and lasting peace. Family members shunned me for exposing the grim truth about our shared history. Like a majority of whites in the Deep South, they preferred to bury the story so that it wouldn't come under public scrutiny, as if the deed itself could be erased by non-exposure. One cousin wrote, "I feel real personal conflict over the idea that the legacy and honor of my father, his brothers and sister, and my grandparents will be defamed and defined by this book as a final remembrance of their lives." Her sense of conflict was one I had struggled with for the duration of the writing.

I felt her pain. Yet non-family readers appreciated the universal themes of racial injustice, oppression, white privilege, repentance, reconciliation and hope, as they played out in a mid-20th century family narrative. That assessment coincided with my motivation to seek out the truth.

For a long time, I drifted in a gray haze, only half hearing what was said to me. I couldn't feel the softness of the couch beneath me. No matter what I ate, it tasted like cardboard. Then in the spring of 2013, a young black man named Gregory Woods, Simon's great-great-grandson, found his way to me via the internet. We forged a connection that resulted in a new relationship to the Delta story. The idiomatic saying, "more will be revealed" resounded in my thoughts as I heard the clear call to pick up the thread of the original story and follow it wherever it led. Three times in the ensuing eighteen months, I travelled to Los Angeles to meet with Gregory and his family. I had no way of knowing that Simon's family would offer me a pathway out of a lingering and uncomfortable state of anxiety, the origin of which resided in my "whiteness," which had cost me nothing yet had given me advantages I did not earn. On a subconscious level, my privilege had stunted my growth as a human being. I learned that oppression of one group of individuals results in a countervailing regression in the oppressors. In order for me to step into my humanity, I would have to own my history, and the racial history of my country. I would need to talk about it, listen to the stories of others and live into the reality. Only then could I get a glimpse at reconciliation from one tiny corner of the world. Gregory and his family provided me with the space and the light, and we started to talk.

In the summer of 2014, a series of horrendous and inexplicable confrontations between black men and the police made the white public newly aware of what black people have known and experienced all along. Advances in technology such as body cameras and cell phones with video capability, evidenced the degree to which our culture is still unsafe for blacks. In each violent incident, the issue of provocation was a negligible factor. Even though all of these clashes resulted in the deaths of black men, the perpetrators (in these cases, the police) were not prosecuted. Outrage on the part of black citizens erupted on city streets. Peaceful demonstrations were carried out in many major cities. Whites walked alongside blacks calling for reform in our criminal justice system. Some media sources reported that we were seeing the worst outbreak of racial violence since the Civil Rights Movement.

At the same time, essays and articles appeared in major news outlets such as *The New York Times* and *The Atlantic Monthly*, calling for reform and suggesting that reparations to black Americans for the years their forbears spent in slavery must be part of a national conversation. When the "Black Lives Matter" movement began to take hold, I heard a clear and persistent call to witness this moment in history. My response has been to return to the work of writing the continuing story of my white family, Simon's black family, and the bonds of charity and benevolence between us over the generations subsequent to the atrocity that brought us together.

And so I began.

Chapter One

OUTRAGE

⟿

"WHERE IS YOUR OUTRAGE?" THIS IS WHAT HE SAID.

These words caught me completely off guard. I had no response except to avert my gaze from his face to the rain-slicked streets intersecting outside the Green Sage Café in downtown Asheville. I took a sip of tepid Chamomile tea to buy some time while I fought the urge to change the subject or discount it altogether.

My friend, Bruce Kennedy, a writer, film-maker, and sculptor had just finished my class in nonfiction writing. The work he'd shared with fellow writers in workshops revealed the creative and principled life of the handsome, tall, bearded and graying white man who'd married Carmen Ramos decades ago after they met in the U.S. Virgin Islands. Together they had two grown daughters living in distant places. He spoke of them with great pride. Not infrequently he would say, "I tell Carmen everything." He wore his love and respect for her as comfortably as the dark gray Ascot cap that warmed his head.

Carmen Ramos-Kennedy had been elected president of the local NAACP in 2015 and was quoted in the Asheville "Citizen –Times" saying, "We're still dealing with issues that the NAACP dealt with at its conception, like the right to vote, equality, equal access to jobs, home loans and mort-gages. It's the same thing that was happening then, but it's a little more shaded now," she added. "We're not dealing with actual lynching, but we are dealing with unarmed black people being shot by law-enforcement."

Because of his interracial marriage and his sensitivity to oppression in our culture, I had given Bruce a copy of *Death in the Delta: Uncovering a Family Secret* and asked him to read it and provide some feedback. The book had been out for a couple of years. I'd spent nearly nine years writing it, and I had experienced a full array of emotions after its release. I felt a measure of pride to have completed the book, a measure of reconciliation and forgiveness, and a degree of freedom for having confronted some of my own demons. Yet there was still a lot I could not explain or answer with regard to my family story. It was just too old—now 65+ years—for there to be living witnesses to the murder cover-up. Regardless of an exhaustive investigation, the final chapter left a number of unanswered questions floating out there like so many kites on a windy day.

When Bruce asked, "Where is your outrage?" I could have said: If I hadn't been impassioned, I would have walked away long before the University Press of Mississippi cranked out the first copy. "Where is your outrage?" I could have responded: If you are referring to my reaction to the injuri-ous and unjust treatment of blacks for centuries, I have to defend myself this way: when I wrote the book I was reeling from the revelation that my Father had participated in the death of two black men.

While I drove back and forth from North Carolina to Mississippi to dig for the truth, I was alone, anxious and afraid of what I would find out. My family had hidden the story and even sixty years later, elder members wouldn't tell me what they knew had happened. This question of Bruce's brought me up short because it indicated that I had left out something of immense importance. There was nothing to do that day except thank him and trudge home feeling deflated, as if I'd failed at what had become my life's most important work. Looking back, I see that I needed more clarification from him, but at the time I was too cowardly to ask for it. Maybe my desire to be balanced in reporting the findings took precedence over my emotions. It had been important not to slant the story. My professional training had emphasized journalistic integrity and adherence to validated facts, even in personal writing, even in memoir. *Death in the Delta* was what's known in the writing world as a "reported" memoir.

Because there hadn't been conclusive evidence about what happened, I had no choice but to close the book with a hypothesis. Little did I know that answers would step out of the shadows, that I would discover not one but two important connections: the existence of Simon's living daughter and her husband, who was the grandson of the cook on my family's plantation. The deep kinship I would forge with Simon's family during the ensuing years, along with a new and public awareness of racial violence, brought me up against the realities of inequality that finally resulted in outrage. How and when did it become acceptable, even habitual, to subjugate a whole race of individuals into a life of suffering, after the long war to free them?

Email dated June 5, 2012

Hello Ms Walling, My name is Gregory Woods and I was talking with my grandmother learning about my family and found out Simon Toombs is my great great grandfather. Doing research I found that you wrote a book about his death. Well, my great grandmother (Simon Toombs's only child) is still alive. My grandmother takes care of her and we would love to learn more about our family.

I felt intrigued that the whisper of a google search led Gregory to seek me out. I wondered about the forces at play in such a seemingly coincidental connection. Then the inner nudge that had sparked my initial curiosity and drive to find meaning in a very old story led me to attempt to re-inhabit the culture of the Mississippi Delta. I felt a growing need to go back there and suss out a more nuanced view.

I DON'T REMEMBER HOW MY FATHER'S BABY BOOK came into my possession but it rests on my desk beside my typing hands, its title embossed in gold: "Baby's Life." Hard to say where my grandmother came across this scrapbook, but it could have been a gift or she might have picked it up in Memphis at Goldsmith's or in Vicksburg, or Greenville, Mississippi. The copyright is 1913 by Barse and Hopkins, so it was printed with now dated drawings of cherubic babies and storks in flight. In 1922, before Dad came into the mysterious and fertile world of the Mississippi Delta, his father, already thirty-eight years old, had set his intention to marry my grandmother, the new teacher at the Anguilla, Mississippi, all-white elementary school where she taught "Expression". She was just twenty years old when she arrived from studying at the Cincinnati Conservatory.

The first photo of Dad was shot in black and white

when he was three days old. Nurse Crouch holds him while she stands in the bright sunshine on the steps of the porch, dressed in a mid-calf length white uniform with white hose, white shoes and a white nurse's cap. She had lived with the couple at Ashland for six weeks prior to Dad's delivery. He was a hefty baby boy, weighing in at eleven pounds. Family narratives reveal that because Thomas had been a bachelor for so long, he was delighted to become a father—protective and doting. God knows what they called Dad until he was four and a half months old, when he was named Harris Jesse Fields (nicknamed "Jay") after his grandfather, who had died six months earlier and who had moved to Mississippi in 1842, before serving in the Confederate Army.

Thomas Walter Fields and my father, Harris Jesse

Upon his return from service to the Confederate Army, Dad's Grandfather, H.J., found that both of his parents had died, his home was gone and he had no money. Two factors worked in his favor. First, the Yazoo-Mississippi Valley cradled some of the most fertile land in the country. Second, he was hard-working and thrifty. Woolfolk plantation, 800 acres, was available for rent. H.J. was soon able to enter an agreement to buy the land for $40,000, and he paid the loan off in five years. In 1866 he married his beloved Martha Catherine who gave birth to my grandfather, Thomas. Martha died in 1904.

During the years between 1904 and 1920, while Thomas and his father were building a small empire, little is known about their personal lives. They lived at Ashland as bachelors, farming, ginning, banking and on occasion, drinking or "letting off steam." I would imagine that the two of them were watching with concern as major events unfolded on the global stage.

In 1913, Anguilla was incorporated, one year prior to the onset of WW I. While race relations may have appeared calm on the surface, underneath blacks were abraded by the inequalities they saw all around them and by the hopelessness they must have felt. WW I set in motion a new wartime economy built on manufacture of artillery, ammunition, and all other necessities of combat. Blacks saw the potential for a less oppressive environment with built-in social mobility due to material enhancements from work that paid well, but it required a move out of the Delta. Thus began the first wave of the Great Migration on those very train rails that had fed the cotton boom. Attrition from the Delta region was slow at first. Though some few blacks found themselves better suited for life in cities like Chicago, New York and

Los Angeles, most stayed "down on the farm." In 1920, one year before Thomas married my grandmother, H.J. gave him 572 acres that comprised Ashland Plantation.

By the time Dad was born, Reconstruction had been over some fifty years and had advanced the position of "colored" folks very little. Marsh, John, Frances and Sarah, along with the field workers on Ashland, would have known that they were still seen as "Mr. Tom's" property though the word "slave" was long out of use. They would not have stretched to exercise newly acquired legal rights because that would have resulted in punishment if not loss of work. After all, in 1865, Mississippi had passed the Black Codes—laws written to circumscribe the mobility and behavior of blacks and to keep them from leasing land so that they were unable to become independent farmers. Workers on Ashland could not own a gun, be idle or disorderly, or use "insulting" gestures. Their children would become "apprentices" until the age of 18.

Southern protocol was evidenced in Tom's and Rebekah's home. His word was law. Rebekah assumed the role of managing domestic help. Black workers bowed to the prevailing Jim Crow system by silently withstanding the demeaning treatment of folks like Mr. Tom and Miss Beck. They wouldn't have dared to "stand up" against it. This was a matter of survival. Tom's approach was paternalistic and involved "the coercion of subordinates through relationships presented as grounded in love" (Maid Narratives 27). He was not inhibited in the use of violence, intimidation or suppression. However, based on stories that were passed down about him, I believe that there was a part of him that was kind, fair and loyal to his workers, and thus he was trusted by them. Their wellbeing was more than a matter of maintaining a labor force.

Rebekah would have enjoyed her role as matron in the household. I have heard that she was loving and protective of her domestics, caring for them as extended family yet ever ready to exploit them for the purposes of perpetuating formality, decency and also for family business profit. She relied on them to follow her example and to strictly adhere to "Southern manners" between the races: always put the happiness and welfare of others first; never be "uppity"; make no public displays of any kind; say please and thank you; don't demand, only ask; always refer to the boss as "sir" and his wife as "ma'am".

In the following photograph, the "help"- Marsh, John, Frances and Sarah -are standing beside the plantation bell. Radios had not been invented by early 1920, but bells played a significant role in communication within each community. Church bells were tolled on Sundays and when there had been a death. Schools had hand bells, and train engines announced approaching stations, arrivals and departures by ringing bells. For entertainment, the phonograph provided music for those who could afford one.

Molly Walling

On the eighteenth of September, 1922, when my Dad was born, the children of Marsh, John, Frances and Sarah might have stepped into their new "separate but unequal" classrooms. In 1921, the town had received a Rosenwald grant (see chapter 14) to build a new school for blacks. The state of Mississippi provided textbooks that the children could pick up at the local drug store, at least until the supply ran out. My Grandfather, Tom Fields, head of the local bank, would have known about this and perhaps contributed to the building of the school. Very few black men could afford to make cash contributions but they did their part in the form of sweat equity.

The family house at Ashland had been built in 1867 by H.J., and it was unremarkable compared to many antibellum homes, but sturdy and capable of handling the thirteen births of H.J. and Martha Catherine's children, then Tom and Rebekah's four. It was a white clapboard, one-story structure with a broad screened-in porch across the front. Upon entering, one encountered the bedrooms on either side of the hall, a living room, a dining room. Meals were carried from the kitchen into the back of the house, where they were served at the dining table. Due to the potential for flooding of the Deer Creek, the house was built on piles.

The Deer Creek Planters Association, of which my great-grandfather was a member, in January 1868 proposed that "Local landlords act collectively to establish uniform wages, hours, and contract terms" (Cobb 58). They proposed a daylight to dark workday with Sundays off for both black laborers and share croppers. What if a black worker lost a job on the plantation? That would mean the loss of income of perhaps as little as $10 a month. How would he or she pay the $4 owed for rent? How would they feed their own children without the kitchen leftovers they brought home after working a 14-16 hour day?

A deep sense of insecurity in white farmers sprang from the need to create and maintain a stable work force. They pushed down harder on the people who most needed change. During the 1880's, improvement in race relations made black labor even more important. Upgrades in the levee system and better access to rail transport like the Illinois Central, increased the value of farmland and cotton prices.

> ...farming in the Yazoo Delta was unlike farming
> in most areas of the country; it was a state of mind.
> No sooner did a man set foot into the Yazoo Delta
> than 'his eyes...opened upon the fair prospect' ...
> This was the infection of the Yazoo Delta. More
> than a place to earn a better living, it represented an
> opportunity to attain the very heights of the South's
> agricultural social status—to be a planter (Cobb 81).

From 1880 on there was an influx of black labor. Anguilla's population rose from 6306 in 1880 to 14,190 in 1920. Thomas and Rebekah were united at an optimal time in terms of prosperity and social status, and as the small town grew, blacks gradually began to see improvements materially and politically. The world market for cotton had expanded, creating a sense of greater potential for gain for planters.

My great-grandfather was able to open a gin and become a founding member of the bank of Anguilla as well as maintain substantial holdings in Anguilla's largest mercantile. His reputation as a war hero and as a planter gave him a mystique that filtered down through the family tree. Personal attributes such as hard work, industriousness, and perseverance, helped to develop a sense of dignity as well as entitlement. Throughout his life, my father tried to emulate his namesake.

Thomas and Rebekah's four children came in the span of seven years. He might have begun to think about limiting the size of his family since he'd witnessed his parents' grief after each of five infants died, but birth control was not available at that time. Some white planters took a black mistress who would have become the primary means of satisfying sexual need.

These liaisons were "not-to-be-spoken-of," yet there were several factors at play that had created an environment in which white men felt entitled to fulfill their physical desires. The availability of black women encouraged commingling of the races and "protected the sexual purity" of white women. Additionally, many white men, raised by black mammies, still sought the "tender and tragic relationship of childhood" (Suddreth 181). But perhaps most importantly, black women dared not resist the advances of their white bosses, lest they risk expulsion from the household and a reputation for being unruly, unreliable, and unfit for hire. According to *The Maid Narratives*, many white men raised two families—one in the front house and one in the back. Even if a black woman had wet-nursed the children in the family she served, she would find no support in the "lady of the house." Wives of planters tended to cast a blind eye on the sexual infidelities of their husbands. It would have been far less acceptable had their men taken up with a white woman in town, especially since the wife's role was Biblical in the sense that she wouldn't oppose or restrain the head of the family. In our clan, there has been little said about Thomas other than that he was devoted to my grandmother, yet he was stern and commanding. If he was angry or just perturbed with someone, Mamaw took the "back seat." This dichotomy of gender roles was part of a deeply established paradigm in the culture of the South.

One of the central unanswered questions in *Death in the Delta* arose from one version of the story that said Simon was killed because he was my father's half-brother—and that he was part owner of our family land. After a title search and countless interviews, I was unable to verify this claim. For it to have been true, Simon's mother, Leana, who was a midwife, might have encountered Thomas while she was assisting in the birthing of a white baby. Had a relationship developed between them, he would have been a twenty-eight or nine year old bachelor when Simon came into the world. But this remains speculative and was never verifiable.

AROUND THE TURN OF THE CENTURY, TWO REMARKable black women moved to Anguilla: Leana Toombs, born in Port Gibson, Mississippi, in 1879, and Mattie Wingate born in 1876 in Louisiana. Their lives soon became inextricably connected to each other and to the Fields family.

In 1911, Shelby Toombs and his wife, Leana, gave birth to a son they named Simon. He was one of six children. Since he was a fair skinned boy, his parentage was suspect. Speculation in the community had it that Simon was born to Thomas Fields, my grandfather. As a young boy, Simon would have been insulated in his family home. There he would have been educated about the realities of growing up in the minority race, in a caste system that severely limited his ability to enhance his life, much less live it without fear of violence. He would have attended church with his family, spending a few hours each week in a safe place where his people had control and self-respect, where he could enjoy the company of other children like him. In 1922, when Dad was born, Simon was 11 years old, enrolled in the black elementary school and at work in the fields alongside his father.

According to the 1920 Census, Mattie Wingate, married to Richard, who spelled his last name Winegate, was living in Anguilla. Little is known about her life before the 1930 Census when she was listed as divorced and as a cook for a private family. Diminutive in stature, neat and tidy in her appearance and dress, Aunt Mat wore glasses and spoke softly and as little as possible. She came to work at Ashland and brought a young boy, Charlie Lee Anderson, with her. He was her grandson, a child whose mother, Vivian Sturdivant, was unfit to raise him. Mat and Charlie Lee would assume important roles in the unfolding story of the Fields family, especially in 1931 when they moved with Tom, Rebekah and their four children to a new home on Highway 61, Anguilla.

A SPECIAL PAGE IN DAD'S BABY BOOK IS DEVOTED

to "mother's notes." Here I found my grandmother's sentiments written the year they moved. September 27, 1931. "H. J. Fields is nine years old today. He is a tall well-built sturdy boy. He has two brothers and one sister. H.J. is kind, loving and honest. He will enter the fifth grade in school. He has many friends and obeys his father and mother." Dad was on his way to becoming a typical Southern "gentleman."

Chapter 2

STORY-TELLING

——◊◊◊——

June 30, 2012

"Ma'am. We don't recommend that our guests go into Compton." So said the uniformed concierge at the LAX Marriott Courtyard when I asked her about cab fares to 130th Street. It was Sunday at 1:00 pm. Only twenty-five days had passed since I received the email from Gregory inviting me to come to L.A. to meet Simon's only daughter and share family history. What made me pay attention to the siren's call? All I can say is that the same curious and yes, reckless, part of me that had to know what really happened in 1946, wouldn't stop egging me on to find out more. My thoughts returned to a phone call from my California daughter warning me to be cautious in L.A. "It's a dangerous city. People are killed there every day." Then I remembered a TV documentary that focused on the Crips and the Bloods, notorious street gangs centered in Compton. Was this an insane idea?

Gregory had said, "Ours is the most beautiful house, well houses in the city. LOL." He planned to be waiting for me at his grandmother's house after attending church. I couldn't let him down. But I took a seat in the lobby for a moment to build up courage for the day ahead of me. Had I flown across the country only to be sidetracked by fear?

The big, burly black cabbie with dreadlocks wound around inside his multi-colored knit beret had a favorite Miles Davis tune playing on the radio. I sized him up as a good guy.

"I'm going to 130th Street, Compton."

"Compton?"

"Yeah why?" I asked.

"Why are you going to meet these people? Did you say you are expected? I'm just not sure if we need to go east or west." Then he assured me that I'd be okay there during the daylight hours and with a clear invitation. We drove on, passing dilapidated houses enclosed within metal fences, with gated driveways and windows with iron bars. Colorful graffiti, cryptic and imposing, graced many of the buildings. The driver began to wax eloquent about the history of the area, explaining that white flight began in the 1940s when blacks started buying up housing and property. Today, the area is a primarily inhabited by Latinos.

He said, "I can't agree with immigration legislation because of places like this. Mexicans come into the country, work hard and then get on public assistance. They move to places like Compton after they learn how to work the system. Lots of drugs, sex trafficking. Americans are working hard to pay for these people." I didn't undertake to correct him about some of his perceptions, which may have been either mistaken or possibly true for reasons other than those he was surely observing.

"Why are you going there?" he casually asked.

I opened up about the book I'd written and told him the whole story line. He listened intently. If I was about to get in trouble in a bad neighborhood, I wanted him to be on my side. Even knowing what I now know and as dedicated as I have become to equality, I still carry old fears, as a privileged white woman. The irony does not escape me.

He stopped by a gated driveway. Two houses, a garage and a workshop were enclosed within the quiet and neat yard, but there wasn't an easily detectable house number. I didn't budge from my seat.

"Go and knock on the door. This has to be the place." The cabbie got out and stood watching me.

"Don't leave me here." Through the gate I went, looking back at the yellow cab.

About that time I heard my name. It was Pat, Gregory's grandmother yelling "Molly!" through the open but curtained window. The next thing I knew, a feisty, fit and toned woman ran from the house and threw her arms around me. I smiled at the sight of her and returned to the cab to gather my belongings. Her black hair was cut in a pageboy, shiny black eyes flickered like rare gems, and flawless warm brown skin shone with a lustrous glow. Pat, exactly my age, looked a good fifteen years younger than me. She wore a short dress with halter top—her biking outfit. Standing in the sunshine on a temperate afternoon, we moved closer into each other's spheres as words marched out of her mouth like a whole squadron of drum majors at the Rose Bowl. She made me feel right at home and totally welcome.

Around 2:30 Gregory and his mother, Latoya, along with Pat and I, were seated at a round table in Pat's kitchen. I had yet to see or hear Virginia, Simon's only child now 81 years old. They offered me a slice of pizza for lunch and a bottle of cold water. At first we talked in an unfocused kind of way, but soon the awkwardness of new acquaintance gave way to a very real sense of friendship. Gregory and Pat were animated and energetic, so I settled in for the long ride back in time. Latoya's quiet self-possession kept us on task.

Gregory, a recent honors graduate from UC Berkeley in Journalism, had his video camera set up and jumped right in, testing out his reporting skills.

"We are here for a round table of discovery of family connection between slave master and the slaves of our families coming together post-civil rights, post slavery and post racism, coming together as one body and one unit to learn more about our families, their lives, their understanding of life and how we can overcome our past to come together in a more unified harmonious future. So we will begin this round table with my grandmother, Patricia Haynes, myself, Gregory Woods, my mother, LaToya Mills and Ms. Walling. And we want to find out if she is family or not. She is the author of the book, *Death in the Delta: Uncovering a Mississippi Family Secret*."

His words, "post-civil rights, post slavery, past racism," took me aback. Later, when I knew him better, I questioned him about his perspective. He said that growing up in L.A., an ethnically diverse city, had given him a more open way of viewing present-day culture.

"Start from the beginning in 2006 with your father and how you came to embark on this journey, which even after the book has been published, you are still finding things and discoveries where you probably wish you could go back and insert some things."

Without hesitation, I began with the family secret. "The story took place after WW II, when there was a confrontation in a juke jive in Anguilla where our families lived. It resulted in the shooting and killing of two men, Simon and

David Jones, both black. The alleged perpetrators were my father, Jay Fields, and his two brothers Tom and Bill. Dad was charged with manslaughter, but was exonerated by an all-white grand jury. There was a cover-up: self-defense. All these years later I had discovered multiple versions of what happened but couldn't resolve it. I learned about the social climate where my family lived and where Simon grew up and about the inter-dependence of these families on each other. It's been a fascinating journey."

Gregory continued, "The perception I got from the book is that the people you thought would help you were the people who made this process a little bit more arduous for you, so could you talk about overcoming the fear of going against your family, the fear of walking into a family that did or did not know the history but who didn't want to talk about what you wanted to talk about. And in an honest light I guess what made you or how did you get over the hump that made you say, 'I can't live in fear no matter what this side of the family says or my side of the family says.'"

Pat broke in, "I didn't know anything until I read your book, not his birthday or anything. I wanted to get a death certificate but I didn't know how because you have to know the name of the parents."

I responded by telling her how I got information from ancestry.com, vital statistics, censuses, military records, the Mississippi Department of Health and first-hand accounts. "From what I know he was born in 1911 in Mississippi and died in December of 1946.

"Here's a photo of Inez Files and Rose Cooper, Simon's nieces," I said. "Inez is truly one of the most wonderful people I've ever met. She encouraged me so much that I got to the point where I thought, 'I can't stop writing because

Inez is counting on me.' Simon's father, Shelby Toombs, was married to Leana, who I learned later had raised Virginia in her home while Simon was away serving in the army for five years during WW II."

Pat said, "That's my mother's grandmother. She was a midwife. And she raised Virginia on the Hall Plantation in Anguilla."

Gregory attempted to get us back on track. "I was wondering if Simon only had one child and it was Virginia, why isn't she mentioned in the book? Why would no one bring her up? Were you shocked when I wrote you saying Simon had a child?"

"Gregory, I made a mistake—his army record says that he did not have any dependents so I believed that and clearly I didn't ask the right questions when I was interviewing Virginia's relatives, because they didn't bring her up either."

Pow. Pow Pow Pow. Loud explosions were going off not far from Pat's house. I reacted by ducking, sensitive to the dangers of the area, even though surrounded by the embrace of this family.

"What is that?" Pat was far less alarmed than I was but looked at Gregory for support.

"Firecracker."

Pat stood up and said, "I'll just go tell Mom that it was a backfire on the street." Pat, Virginia's sole caregiver, was vigilant and careful with her mother. I was not yet aware that Virginia was sequestered in the first house on the property, bedridden and alone.

Latoya had remained quiet and focused but she let me know that she had been fascinated with her family's history for many years. When she was in middle school, she told Simon's story to her classmates and teacher. I asked her to retell it, as it had been related to her.

"Yes, it was originally orated by my mother (Pat) and what I did was put it in a speech form and acted it out. I put drama to it. It was because of the way she told the story, the emotion of it came across. There was a lot of practicing with me in the 7th grade. I won the speech. Later I came to appreciate it more because it hit me that this is my family, this wasn't something or someone that I had read a book about or learned about on TV. It was a story that took root in my own family tree so I did come to appreciate it even in middle school. When I had to do the speech it was Black History Month, and we could pick whatever topic we wanted to pick, and I told Mom and she said, 'You should write about your great grandfather, Simon Toombs.' So then she started telling me the story. That he was a decorated military man."

Gregory interrupted her. "Simon and the Fields Brothers knew each other and one night when he came home from the war and he had survived of course and he had been coming home late from a bar, he ran into the Fields brothers and they were drunk and they were telling him—'you're uppity because you have on your army jacket, and so they taunted him about being uppity but they were drunk. Simon had chastised them because they were pointing a gun at him, telling him to crawl and he said, 'I'm not going to crawl, I fought for this country. I'm not going to come home just to crawl or run. I'll walk but I'm not going to run.' So words took place and he was shot until he crawled. He got shot, he kept getting back up, he wouldn't crawl so they shot him until he was completely dead. So the honor in that is that until the time he died he never crawled and he died in an honorable way for his country."

Pat returned from reassuring her mother. She broke in and retold the story just as Latoya and Gregory had. She explained that according to her sources, Dad, Tom and Bill were not drunk. They were just out on the town and angry … "because all the blacks would get together when they got back (from work) and go to the juke joint and then after they had enough, they all go home and so they was leaving the juke joint and that's when the brothers came up and approached them. I guess he didn't do what he was supposed to and they was agitated."

As old as this story had become, sixty-eight years, many versions were held captive in people's memories. Simon's death had become a hero's tale, a story of mythic proportions. How does a family make peace with the horror of it? One way is by glorifying the dead. Simon's refusal to degrade himself at the behest of three white men attests to the growing insurgency amongst black farm workers. It cost him his life just after he had proven himself in service to the country. He did indeed die, in a sense, "for his country."

Pat said, "I met two of the Fields brothers before Aunt Mat (Virginia's mother-in-law) died. They was in a charter plane. Bill had a plane, and she was in a wheel chair and he said, 'Oh, Mama's worried about you and told me to come see about you and see how you are doing.' She said, 'I'm doing fine' and she gave him a hug. He was nice and I said he doesn't look like a killer. He looks like a regular guy. I mean, I said, Wow. He just seemed very sincere with her and said, 'I had to come check on you because Mama told me to.'"

Uncle Bill did have a private plane at one time. He and Aunt Lib enjoyed flying to the coast and points beyond. I knew how devoted my grandmother had been to Aunt Mat, who cooked for her and helped to raise my Dad and his siblings. It was heartening to know that Mamaw had sent the boys to check on Mat.

I attempted to get back to the incident, adding that my uncle, Tom, had been shot in the shoulder during the confrontation at the Pan Am. "According to King Evans, a ninety three year old witness to the killings, they went to town to shut down the Pan Am station where there was a coloreds-only bar. King said, 'I don't know how they thought they had the authority to shut down the juke joint and why didn't they go to the proprietor and not to the people that were there.'"

Pat returned to the issue of bearing firearms. "But I don't think that blacks back then would shoot at nobody. They didn't go around like that. They couldn't. They'd get arrested. They wouldn't want to jeopardize causing an upheaval. They just wanted to have fun and the other three wanted to have fun too but probably in a different way."

I interrupted her, "Let me ask—this is important here - how did you get this story Pat?"

"Grandmama Lilly and my granddaddy—remember I showed you, the white one—he and his wife - my grand-mother who raised me, the only grandmother I knew. Mama Lilly and him. They were both raised in Anguilla. They got married in Anguilla and came out here and that's when he said, 'I'm smart.' He bought three houses and he sent for my Dad and got him one (a house) but Dad messed up, started gambling and stuff. When my dad came out here, this was fast for them, so they didn't know how to slow down, it kind of sucked them up."

I remembered that while Pat and I waited for Gregory and Latoya to come, she showed me a photograph of a distinguished looking black man with pale, olive skin and blue eyes. He and his wife migrated to L.A. in 1944. Because he was not discernibly black, he was hired by the railroad and thus began a period of prosperity that allowed him to purchase property. Two years later, Simon was shot, leaving fourteen year old Virginia bereft and alone in the care of her grandmother. By the time she was sixteen, Virginia had fallen in love with Charlie Lee Jr., and she had become pregnant.

Gregory asked, "When he came here with Grandma Virginia, they were married?"

"Yeah, they were married," Pat responded.

While Gregory and Pat collaborated on family history, I was distracted and caught up in the story Latoya had started and Greg had finished. The details of Simon's encounter with my Dad and his brothers were breathtakingly painful to assimilate into the versions I had become accustomed to telling.

When I found an entryway into the conversation, I said, "I just can't get over what you said about Simon not running and they kept shooting him."

Pat said, "That's what both of them told me, granddaddy and Mama Lilly. I guess the town knew that—the black folks probably knew that. They told it amongst themselves because back then everything had to be hush hush. You had to be careful about what you said, you'd be killed or lynched." Fear in the black community was so strong that it overpowered the urge to retaliate on behalf of the dead and their families. Renditions of what happened circulated behind color lines.

Gregory wanted to return to the issue of guns. "What was the climate like after WWII? I think the climate thing sounds more appropriate before WWI. I'm just thinking

Molly Walling

that a black man coming back from the army isn't going to have a gun."

"No," Pat stressed, "That gun is given to you in war but not to take home. It's taken back. They don't give you a gun to take home. They didn't have access to guns there."

I thought about the disparities in the stories about Simon and David carrying guns. For me, it was entirely tenable that they were unarmed. Pat was right that the army would not have allowed servicemen to carry army issued guns once they were back in civilian life. My aunt had said that there were stabbings at the juke joint and that our family had transported field workers to the doctor because of the violence that broke out, but she didn't mention shootings. The scar on my uncle's shoulder, however, was proof that someone else had a weapon besides the Fields men.

"Why would Dad want to shut down a tavern anyway if he could go to the proprietor and ask him to shut it down? Why didn't he go to the police or the sheriff? Because the sheriff was getting paid off—it was bootleg alcohol." I didn't want to go deeply into the fact that blacks had so little protection under the law. It wasn't time to discuss the nuances of oppression that led people like Charlie Lee Sr. to migrate out of the South.

Latoya spoke. "There needed to be a whole generation of change before my family would see any improvement in their lives."

I responded to her. "In a sense the black men coming back from serving in the war had almost been catapulted into the next century. They had been given uniforms and guns; they were going out to serve the country just like white men. They saw what was possible for them—that they could have equal treatment. That was a huge thing."

Pat said. "So the white people was threatened about them coming and having an ego. 'I don't have to say yessum and nossir no more.' That would have been a horrific change for them (whites) in that area and they didn't want that change. They wanted to have control."

Gregory added, "I heard that there was a war on two fronts. So for the black man —a war abroad and a war at home. According to the rumors you heard in Mississippi, did you ever figure out if you were related to Simon? or not related?'

Boom. Boom. Boom. Shattering blasts rattled me and disrupted our conversation.

Gregory must have sensed my discomfort. " You know, L.A. is next to Tijuana and you go get fire crackers."

"Yeah but I don't like that," Pat said, "I'm gonna call Junior and tell them to stop that. Well, the police gonna start comin' out. They can hear it and they gonna start searchin' with the helicopter."

The time had come for us to talk about that rumor that surfaced while I was writing *Death in the Delta*. Racial commingling was and still is a taboo subject in white society in the Deep South. My exposure of it in my first book had been repugnant to my family and many had disowned me for writing about it. "The story was that Simon was my father's half-brother and that means that his mother had to have had a relationship with either my grandfather or my great grandfather. I was told that the reason why they wanted to kill Simon was because he had been given some land."

Gregory said. "Oh man I was reading those pages like —what? I'm related to this man? This is crazy. You ever read so long your eyes started hurting? But I couldn't put the book down because I wanted to know, did she figure it out? This is juicy stuff. The thing that made me so mad—I think it's your aunt." Gregory said, "I feel like she knows."

Latoya looked me in the eye and said, "So you never confirmed?"

"I...." Then Gregory finished my sentence for me.

"Tried hard. I could tell from the book."

This topic was difficult for me. "The problem, Pat, was that if there was a relationship and land was at the heart of the struggle... there could have been an oral gift. 'You are my son, I'm going to give you some land.' I went through all the records and there was no sign of a written deed."

Pat replied. "They wouldn't let anything get exposed like that because he (Dad or one of his brothers) would have to live with that. For you, that question mark will always be there, 'I wonder.'"

Gregory pointed to his grandmother. "But what about her (Pat's) mother, because she's a direct descendent of Simon Toombs." He was referring to the possibility of genetic testing.

"That's right. It's something we need to think about. Dad may not have pulled the trigger. It could have been Bill." I knew by then that my uncle's family would literally rather die than participate in a DNA test.

Pat nodded vigorously. "My dad said it was Bill. My daddy said it was Bill. My Dad, Charlie Lee Anderson, said it was Bill."

Latoya smiled. "Wouldn't it be something if we was really all related? It was pretty common that nobody wanted those secrets out but from everything that I read, the men were pretty nurturing to their kids because that's their blood and those children would get better jobs in the house, and they were dealt with a little bit more leniently. The wives felt disgraced. It happened but you did not talk about it at all."

"My dad was a writer; he was in journalism." I looked at Gregory and smiled.

At last Latoya addressed her thoughts. "If we had a chance to check DNA—that would be nice to know."

Pat deflected the issue of paternity by changing the subject. I was afraid to push that agenda so soon in our relationship, but it floated out there on the horizon. I wasn't ready to suggest that we get serious about genetic testing. The result of the time I spent with Pat, Gregory and Latoya was remarkable in the sense that their understanding of what happened December 12, 1946, was relatively congruent with my research. Sixty some years later, Simon's legacy was alive and well in his extended family. This family, strong in its faith, in its love, in its acceptance of me, was one I wanted to get to know better.

Molly, Pat, Latoya and Gregory
in Los Angeles, June 2013.

Molly Walling

Chapter 3

VIRGINIA

·····⟨≈≈⟩·····

Eighteen years after the start of the California Gold Rush, the city of Compton was settled. The year
was 1867. The area was known as Hub City because of its
location in the exact center of Los Angeles. Many of the
pioneers who settled there had travelled south as the gold
mines depleted. Originally part of Ranchero San Pedro,
the land was inhospitable and hard to cultivate, but with
determination, the settlers prospered and the city grew and
matured with a predominantly white populace. Eventually
the streets were lined with single family homes, and middle
class blacks were attracted to Compton. Until the late 40s,
people, however, with a non-Caucasian background were
discouraged from moving there. The prevailing perception
was that if blacks began to move in, property values would
plummet. Restrictive covenants were established. Eventually the middle class suburban community encompassed
ten square miles and had a population of 100,000.

While Simon was serving in the army, in 1944, Charlie
Lee Anderson, Sr. left the Delta with his wife, Lilly, headed
for Chicago, leaving his fourteen-year-old son, also named
Charlie Lee, in the care of Aunt Mat on my family's plantation. In all likelihood, they rode north on the Illinois

Central railroad. What prompted their departure? In *The Warmth of Other Suns*, historian Isabel Wilkerson addresses this question by saying that we can only speculate about the motivations that rural, southern blacks had for leaving their homes, families and all that was familiar to them when they moved into the North, Midwest and West during the years of the Great Migration, but the impetus could have been better wages, or better living, an effort to fight off a heavy malaise brought on by living in the South, or it could have been an impulse to survive.

Pat told me that Charlie Lee didn't find Chicago to his liking and heeded the advice of a relative to go to California. Wilkerson says,

> They would cross into alien lands with fast, new ways of speaking and carrying oneself and with hard-to-figure rules and laws. The New World held out higher wages but staggering rents that the people had to calculate like a foreign currency. The places they went were big, frightening, and already crowded—New York, Detroit, Chicago, Los Angeles…(9).

> More colored people migrated to California in the 1940s than had come in all the previous decades put together. (187)

Fortunately for Charlie Lee Sr., the move west was fortuitous. At that time, railroads in California were not hiring blacks, but Charlie Lee's skin tone was pale enough and his eyes blue enough that he could pass for white. He was hired on by the railroad, started saving his money, and ultimately bought three houses in Compton. At that time over one third of blacks in L.A. owned their homes. He would have been in the minority living there in the mid-to-late 1940s, but over the next three decades the area lost its gentry, many to the hillside towns surrounding L.A. In the next half century, Compton saw affluent residents continue to come and then go. The area fell into decline as property values did, indeed, fall.

I questioned my own negative perceptions about that part of Los Angeles. In a 2009 *Newsweek* article by Jessica Bennett, I found some answers. "By the 1990s, the mere mention of the name Compton had become so toxic that the nearby southern California suburbs had the city of 100,000 erased from their maps. Its schools were crumbling. Drugs were rampant, and street-gang tensions had escalated into what historian Josh Sides describes as 'a brutal guerilla war.'"

So as not to be insulting to my new friend, I gingerly broached the subject of safety in Compton. Pat resisted my notion that the area was still dangerous. Even though poverty and unemployment figures are high, murders occur much less often. The city is now 70% Latino. Maybe the most important factor in the rejuvenation of Compton was the presence of community activists like Pat, neighborhood crime watches and church leaders who maintain a good relationship with the sheriff's department.

Gregory, Latoya, Pat and I talked late into the after-noon. They pored over photographs and documents that I brought from home—all relating to Simon and their family members. Pat photocopied many of them. Gregory was cap-tivated by a picture of my grandparents' home. I mentioned to him that the driveway wound to the right and back of the house where there was an alley along which fifteen shotgun houses were inhabited by folks like his Aunt Mat before she moved to California.

"Shot gun houses!" The term was new to him. Aunt Mat's house would have been about twelve feet wide with one room leading to another with no indoor plumbing in the earliest constructed houses. My grandmother told me that the name came from the notion that a bullet fired in the front door could travel straight through and exit through the back.

Pat began to talk about Mat or "Otta" with loving words. "She was a strong, feisty woman, and she didn't want daddy to do nothing wrong when he was livin' in that house. I never seen my daddy show so much affection as he did towards Otta. He was really protective of her."

I produced a photograph of my family that was taken around the time of Simon's death. "Dad was twenty-four when Simon was shot."

"I'm twenty four." Gregory said in a reflective tone.

Latoya changed our focus. "Of all the history books I've read, books by slaves who wrote their own stories, it was pretty common that masters had kids with slaves. They were okay with it, but the wives were ashamed. The fathers were trying to nurture as much as they could, because their kids would be different and would be shunned by other kids."

Gregory interrupted her. "That's where the one drop rule came from." Historically, the colloquial term "one drop rule" was used to designate any person with even one drop of African American blood in his or her DNA as Negro. The rule was passed into law in the twentieth century. The issue of skin color was one that had confounded me since I first started writing. While I was doing research in Mississippi and throughout the succeeding years, I frequently heard blacks talk with each other about skin color as a point of pride or of derision. In *Men We Reaped,* Jesmyn Ward writes about growing up in Alabama. "We are conscious of the way bloodlines are so entangled in our community, so much so that back in the early 1900s, adults in DeLisle would arrange visits with other communities of mixed-race people in Alabama or Louisiana to match children with marriageable mates to vary the gene pool (10)." The fact that Charlie Lee Sr. was so light skinned he could pass for white was and still is regarded as a strong indicator of self-worth. "Colorism" is unfortunately still relevant in black communities.

Latoya continued, "I was just saying that it was pretty common that nobody wanted those secrets out but from everything that I read, the white men were nurturing to their kids. It was the wives that were selling the kids off to other farms and getting rid of them. It happened but you didn't talk about it at all. It might make sense that the rumor from the attorney was that your dad was the one who might have known that Simon was in the family. I really want to follow that—if we had a chance to check DNA—that would be nice to know."

In truth I was unprepared to open that door all the way because as long as I didn't know whether we were "kin", I didn't have to think about what it might mean. I wasn't ready to accept the fact that one of the men in my family might have taken advantage of Simon's mother. That Latoya pushed for DNA testing didn't settle on my heart until I was back home in Asheville. She and Gregory let me know by words and body language that they hoped we were connected that intimately. This gesture on their part was a gift of immense proportion. How could it be that they hoped to be related to the man that took the life of their forefather? First they welcomed me into their home. They shared their stories with me. Now this, another act of tender mercy.

Gregory remembered his great-grandmother and said, "Let's go see her."

We walked outside into the temperate, sunny air of southern California. Gregory and Latoya commented on how much they loved living in Los Angeles and wouldn't ever want to leave it. From Pat's house we ambled toward the front of the property where the small white bungalow faced the street. The sun was approaching the horizon. One room appeared to be dimly lit. Inside, we found eighty-one-year old Virginia propped up in her hospital bed. Degenerative bone disease had nearly devastated her tiny body. Her feet curled under so that they would no longer bear her weight. Her vertebrae and discs were twisted out of alignment. The subtleties of her confinement began to dawn on me. Since she was unable to walk, Virginia had to maneuver her body to the portable toilet next to the bed. She ate the three daily meals that Pat prepared for her and spent the rest of her day working crossword puzzles and watching TV. Lined up along the windowsill were packs of cigarettes. Pat rationed them, and she dealt with constant requests for alcohol. Only on special occasions would she allow her mother a glass of wine. With pride, Pat told me that those requests were coming with less frequency.

Any needs Virginia had, would have to be met by Pat. Trips to the hairdresser and doctors depended solely on her, yet Pat didn't indicate the slightest dissatisfaction with her role as caregiver. Now retired after working thirty-four years in grocery stores like Lucky's and Albertson's, she had the time to devote to her mother.

When Simon died, Virginia was only fourteen years old, a formative time in the life of a young girl approaching womanhood. I would imagine that a loss so tragic and brutal would have overwhelmed Virginia's capacity to cope. Trauma at her young age would have created in her body a response to certain triggers. Throughout her life, whenever she felt a loss of control, a sense of having someone exercise power over her, when she felt defenseless, she might react in ways that mimicked her early experience of losing her father. It is not unfair to assume that Virginia would have had a hard time trusting people and that the unpredictability of life would forever throw her off kilter. What I found that afternoon in 2013 was a woman whose life in that bedroom was circumscribed by the toll a life-changing event inflicted on her body, yet there she was, alive, mentally alert, happy to have company.

She was gracious and loving toward her family, and she accepted me because of them. When we gathered around her bed, Virginia greeted each of us with a broad smile. Gregory tried to make her more comfortable by situating the fan so that she felt its cooling effects in a room that had to have been in the upper 80s. He said, "It feels like a desert in here. I don't know how you stand it."

Latoya asked her grandmother why her father, Simon, and her grandmother raised her and not her own mother.

Virginia responded, "My dad took me from my mama cause she was a party girl."

"They drank heavily," Pat said. "Like you sing the blues? They tried to make the blues go away with alcohol and it didn't work." Virginia didn't answer. Pat's candor with her was surprising. Over time I would come to see how the two had developed a remarkable relational dance. Virginia became childlike and coy to get what she wanted. Pat used humor when she had to set boundaries. Once when Virginia tried to wheedle a glass of wine out of Pat, she told her, "the doctor said I could have a drink." Pat's response was typical. "The doctor… he died."

I asked her, "How old were you when Simon died?"

"Just a child."

"Do you remember when he died?"

"No. I remember the whole town after it happened. I don't remember who told me. I was told my daddy was killed by the Fields brothers. It was like a shock. They didn't expect nothing like that. A war hero just comin' back and gettin' started. Nobody expected it. It was just a bad thing that happened in Anguilla. My grandmother, Leana, was in shock but she wouldn't let me see her like that. She kept strong. She stayed strong so I would stay strong."

Gregory asked, "Do you know why the Fields brothers went to shut down the bar?"

"They didn't have nothing else to do. They was bored and didn't have nothing else to do but go mess with somebody else and that was it."

These words evoked complex emotions within me. I had heard so many versions of what had happened December 12, 1946, but this was not one of them. If she had said these words with anger, it would have been easy for me to discount them, but she made this statement with absolute resolve. I had to admit to myself that there was some likelihood that she was right, just as there may have been at least a grain of truth to other accounts. Even though I have accepted the culpability of my Father, I still want to believe, based on my experience of him, that he had a moral compass, but these words of Virginia's tested the limits of my need to believe that my father had a good heart. Was it possible that he took a life because he was bored? To so devalue a human life, regardless of race, is even more abominable than striking out in rationalized self-justifying anger.

Virginia's bedroom was austere and simple with few trappings, but hanging on the wall near her bed was a framed picture of an African American soldier in his olive drab uniform. It was Simon. In his face I saw pride, dignity and youth. It brought me to tears. This image of Virginia's father was an ever present reminder to her. It brought her happy memories yet also loss and immense sadness. I looked at Virginia and mustered all the strength I had before saying, "I'm just really sorry that you had to live your life without your dad."

She said, "That was the hard part."

Pat reminded her mother that she had been a writer of stories and poetry. "That's all she did. Write, write, write." This information about Virginia surprised me. My prejudicial thinking didn't allow much room for the notion that women of her generation had much time to spend on creative pursuits, and I doubted that they had the education necessary to write prose, even though I had read and admired the works of black women writers like Alice Walker, Maya Angelou, Toni Morrison, Toni Cade Barbara and Zora Neale Hurston. That's how ignorant I was in some unreconstructed corner of my unconscious.

"I would love to read some of Virginia's stories," I said when Gregory interrupted.

" She had books everywhere. She read some of them over and over."

"We had no TV so a book was like my TV in those days." Virginia later told me about getting the Book of the Month Club selections in the mail. She waited for them to arrive, and it felt like Christmas when they did, especially if they were mysteries.

Before we left Virginia, I told her again how sorry I was that her father died the way he did and when she was so young. She didn't respond. It was gravely important to me that my apology would register with Virginia, that she would hear it and take it in. Her silence registered as a refusal to accept my words but later, after we left her house, she told Pat that she thought I was a sincere person. It occurred to me that Virginia, and probably most blacks, couldn't trust a middle class white woman. I was a cliché, a person representing an ethos that had undermined the best efforts of oppressed people who were trying hard to survive in an unfair world. Why would she trust me? And I was family to the men who murdered her father.

After the events of the long and intense afternoon, I was staggering with fatigue. Pat and Gregory drove me back to my hotel near LAX. I said good-bye reluctantly, as this family had been so kind to me. My hope was that I had provided them with ancestry material they would enjoy having. The poignancy and intimacy of the afternoon was a gift to me.

Though he was intensely focused on our visit, Gregory had future plans to think about. His recent graduation from UC Berkeley had instilled enormous pride in this family because he was the first to receive a college education. With the Master's Degree in Journalism, awarded to him summa cum laude, he prepared to attend media job fairs that would help him find employment. His hard work paid off. The ABC affiliate in Charleston, South Carolina, was to become his first assignment as a working reporter. He would, after all, have to leave his beloved family and friends behind, at least for a while.

PAT'S FOND MEMORIES OF OTTA SPARKED ONE OF MY own. During a long ago visit to my Grandmother's home in Mississippi, Aunt Mat took me to her house. The bare walls were covered with greeting cards from her family in California. She expressed great pride as she told me about their accomplishments. Mat's formal education was minimal. She learned to read by studying the Bible. Most blacks in the Deep South were discouraged from going to school—not just because they would be needed to work in the fields and around the plantation, but because their employers feared the effects of an enlightened mind. It might lead to aspirations of a better life. They might come to know and resent the qualitative difference in their lives and those of affluent whites. In *Trouble in Mind* , Leon Litwack further explains that, "to be educated was to be somebody, to proceed beyond a rudimentary education, as parents and employers recognized, was to invite higher aspirations and ambitions than agricultural labor "(57).

The seasons of agricultural life made schooling a near impossibility. In the fall, up until Christmas, children worked in the fields picking cotton alongside their parents. After the holidays, the school year would commence but only for about three months when temperate weather brought the kids back to the fields to chop cotton, pull vines and drive the tractor. For three months a year, black children were taught about personal hygiene, home economics and survival.

Aunt Mat moved to California in the 1970s. She was there when Gregory was born, and she would have been delighted to learn that he had been schooled far beyond anyone else in the family. But that's not all she would have loved about him. In Anguilla, Mat was known for her faithful participation in her church. Undoubtedly her ability to cope and stay the course in the dark days of the Jim Crow South were fueled by her ability to look up to a source of strength far greater than herself.

As Christians, African Americans could spiritually, if not physically, resist the powers that be. After emancipation African American worshipers sought to reconcile the contradictions and oppression in the social environment. Worship was directed to a God who had experienced suffering, just like they had. Jesus promised them rest from their labor, an end to injustice, and eternal punishment for the violent and oppressive" (Clark-Lewis 34).

Pat, Latoya and Gregory knew that kind of omnipotent power, and they worshipped regularly.

In numerous Facebook postings, Gregory revealed his intimate connection to his God. Here's one example:

Email dated 10/9/13

> *Was at bible study earlier with all men...& seeing men not ashamed of the Gospel reminded me how powerful it is when men of God stop acting like punks & be a soldier for the Lord.*

Chapter 4

DISPARITIES

⸺∽∽∽⸺

AFTER I RETURNED TO ASHEVILLE FROM L.A., I decided to look deeper into my family's history for a more subtle understanding of the dynamics of black/white relations that existed in the Jim Crow culture of Mississippi and other southern states. It was important to shake myself loose from the notion that interdependence could outweigh blatant inequality.

In 1924 when Dad was two years old, his parents produced another baby boy, Tom. Then in May of 1926, a third son, Bill, was born to Rebekah and Thomas. He arrived late in planting season and kept the couple purposefully occupied. Farming life had a heartbeat of its own, one that could not be interrupted short of natural disaster. During the first summer of Bill's life, the rain began to fall on the Delta and indeed, throughout the Midwest. The Army Corps of Engineers had constructed a levee system along the banks of the Mississippi River between 1913 and 1926. Those in command supported a "levees-only" policy when it came to containment of the mighty waters. John M. Barry points out in his seminal work, *Rising Waters*, that the levees were fortress-like. "The crown was flat, at least 8 feet wide, and the sides had a three-to-one slope, so a levee 30 feet high would be at least 18ft wide....The entire levee was planted with tough-textured and thickly rooted Bermuda grass to hold the soil"(190).

The system appeared to be working well until this particular rainy season started and didn't stop. On the morning of Good Friday, 1927, Rebekah, Thomas and the children would have been safely nestled in their home on Ashland. On that day the rainfall reached torrential proportions and continued rising in the Mississippi until the pressure on the levees began to threaten their stability. Already the rainfall had surpassed its yearly annual average by tenfold or more. In thirty-six hours, levees began to give way one after another until the river broke through in 145 places. In the end, 27,000 square miles of acreage had been subsumed by the waters of the Mississippi River.

Thomas would have realized the dangers that faced his family if they remained at home. He had subscribed to the Sunday *New York Times*, which carried the story of flooding throughout the middle of the U.S., but newspapers closer to home and friends around the Delta would have kept him apprised day by day so that he acted in a timely way, packed up my grandmother, the three boys and Aunt Mat, and got them to the train station in time for a departure to someplace in Ohio, well out of harm's way.

I think about what it would have been like for Rebekah to leave Thomas, fearing for his safety, her home and kinfolks left behind. Segregated train travel probably meant that Mat was subjugated to a coloreds only car, but accounts of the flood indicate that a disaster of this magnitude diminished the hard lines between the races when they just needed to survive by working together. Maybe Mat was allowed to ride with Rebekah since she traveled with three little boys four years old and under.

Back in Anguilla, Thomas had plenty to do to prepare as best he could for the onslaught of water. Whatever furniture and belongings he could get to storage on a second story, he removed with the help of servants. He had to have the field workers and house servants on his mind because the water, at its height, swept away all but the sturdiest structures along with dead animals like cows, mules and dogs, trees snapped off at ground level, untethered rooftops, etc. He was among the fortunate in that he had a boat and so was able to assist others, some of whom climbed onto the tin roofs of their shacks or high into trees. The *Jackson Clarion-Ledger* reported that "… there is not the slightest doubt… that several hundred Negro plantation workers lost their lives in the great sweep of water" (Barry 202). Those fortunate enough to see the rain stop, were bereft of everything unless they moved their meager belongings onto the levee top where a miles-long refugee camp was established and provisions and aid were brought in by the Red Cross. Many blacks were displaced for six months or longer. Many left the Delta and headed north. The Great Flood had increased the ranks of the Great Migration.

After the floodwaters subsided, Thomas put the black help to work restoring the home place on Ashland. There was muck and stench everywhere in the house and outside. As described in *Rising Tide*

> The cleanup seemed endless and hopeless. Mud was caked everywhere, four to eight inches of the alluvial deposits that had created the Delta. It gave off a thick, fetid smell, a smell like dung mixed with swamp gas. Rattlesnakes, water moccasins, frogs, insects and spiders infested the buildings. The rot of death was everywhere (328).

It must have taken weeks to salvage what they could of the life they had known. But Thomas would not have allowed Rebekah to come home until some semblance of normalcy had been restored.

She, the children and Aunt Mat arrived safely back in Anguilla from Ohio, and soon after, Thomas was absorbed in plans to build a fitting home, one that would be sound and impervious to natural disaster. An architect from Kentucky was employed to draft the two story red brick house. In two years' time, the project was complete. Despite the fact that Wall Street had crashed in 1929, Thomas realized his dream, moving his family, including a new baby girl, into "Greenfields" in 1931. The new house was situated on the property facing Highway 61, which was the route from Memphis to New Orleans. In time it would become known as the Blues Highway because it was the road blacks took to find a better life. Songs written about the route helped to establish black music as a significant contribution to our nation's cultural heritage.

"Greenfields"

On the ground floor, a guest at the home would enter the gracious foyer that rose to the height of the second story. With wainscoting, a dark wood sideboard and an oriental rug, the space was large enough to accommodate a winding staircase. When we visited, my siblings and I waited for our grandmother to tackle one of her projects so we could scamper up the stairs and slide down the banister. There was hell to pay when she discovered what we were doing. To the right of the foyer was the living room with a fireplace nestled between tall bookcases topped with arched shells, painted white. Further in that direction was the sunroom. To the left, one entered a large dining room with banquet table and chairs, a massive crystal chandelier hanging overhead. Off that room was the sun porch. And toward the rear of the house there was a breakfast room off the kitchen on one side and a guest bedroom and bath on the other. The family drove under the *porte cochere* and entered through the back of the house. Upstairs, four bedrooms, two baths, a sewing room were in constant use by Thomas, Rebekah and the children.

Rebekah found herself needing more and more help as her family grew. She hired Josephine Matlock to help keep the house clean and Mat continued to work in the kitchen. They lived in shotgun houses across the back alley. Aunt Mat was deeply religious and seldom missed a Sunday at church. She was strong and highly respected in the black community. Clearly, her faith and regular church attendance enhanced her self-respect. I believe it is fair to say that Mat didn't accept the white-imposed restrictions placed on her but rather chose to work within them and consequently, she triumphed over them and more importantly, she survived. When I asked my brother, Jay, the oldest of Rebekah and Thomas' grandchildren, what he remembered about Aunt Mat, he said, "When I think of her, I mostly think of an attitude that goes like this— 'Yes, I'll do whatever I need to do to keep things running around here but just for the record, you are not in charge of who I am as a person and don't forget it.' In other words she seemed to be considerably her own woman." I was too young when I knew her to have made such an astute observation, but I do remember feeling safe around her, cared for and loved.

Mat was alive when the Southern Railroad came through Anguilla and when the bank and post office were in the same building. In 1929, electric power came to Sharkey County so Thomas was able to install a DELCO lighting system in the new home and then hook up with Mississippi Power and Light.

Thomas made certain that Rebekah had everything she needed to keep her happy and to keep her home in good working order. With a house full of young children, ages two to nine, abstinence was the only reliable birth control method. From time to time he slipped off for a few days of "blowing off steam." He took the "house boy" John Parks and drove the short distance down Hwy 61 to Ashland for a few days of heavy drinking. He was even known to have strayed as far away from home as Memphis, driving there in his Rickenbacker, one of only 35,000 such autos built between 1922 and 1927. Most people could not afford the stylish coupe so eventually the company was forced to shut down. Thomas' longer trips away from home necessitated an expensive piece of jewelry for Mamaw.

She took to the planters' life in the Delta with aplomb. She was a large woman, imposing and comfortable with her power. Jay described her to my daughter this way: "Mamaw ruled the family. She was a big woman, physically and in most other ways, and I'd say it was pretty much her way or the highway. I liked her because there was always such falderol going on around her all the time. You didn't just drink tea, it had to be a certain way, out of a certain glass (usually amber), and with a sprig of mint. And you had to drink it on the porch in certain chairs in the afternoon when there was just the slightest breeze stirring on the Delta."

Those folks that lived on the home place, that worked in the yard, in the house, in the fields, were considered "part of the family" but more in the sense of being property, being owned. Mamaw knew the quirks of personality and the gifts of the people she claimed as her own. She readily shouldered responsibility for getting the sick to a doctor, for rallying the spirits of those going into the three-month harvest period. They depended on her to watch their backs and it was part of a mutual, intimate contract of loyalty. But, as noted, its success hinged upon a separate and unequal status quo. Noblese oblige, although considered to be obligatory for a person of my grandmother's status, was demeaning. In a newspaper article written about Rebekah in 1981, the interviewer writes,

> At Ashland (and later Greenfields) there were always cooks, maids, gardeners and helpers of all types. Mrs. Fields didn't realize how dependent she was on them, … until one day she realized she didn't know how to operate the timer on her oven. Always before, she had prepared her special dish and handed it to the cook to put in the oven.

When Mamaw was preoccupied in the house, my father and his siblings often played with neighboring children but when that was not possible, they recruited Charlie Lee Jr. into their games and antics. Seven years younger than Dad, he was born in 1930 and grew up with his grandmother, Aunt Mat. His father had already left the Delta for California. Mat kept an eye on Charlie Lee and made sure he minded, especially when Mamaw was around. Undemonstrative, Mat was austere and rarely affectionate. A woman of few words, she directed the activities of her grandson, making sure he did his work and did it well. When he was allowed to play, he joined Dad and the others in games of Kick the Can, Crack the Whip, and baseball. My father once told me that a favorite activity was to dig a good sized hole, fill it with brush, set it afire with sweet potatoes nestled under another layer of brush. This made for a healthy snack.

They got into trouble too. Not necessarily Charlie Lee, but Dad and his brothers were up to no good much of the time. For example, they destroyed the neighbors' mailboxes by bashing them to smithereens with baseball bats. No doubt Charlie Lee got to know the boys' personalities very well. Like most black children with little to-no-education, he had to learn the protocol of plantation life by observation and stern guidance from Mat. She would have made certain that he was deferential in his dealings with the Fields family, adults and children alike. I have often wondered if Charlie Lee spoke of the Fields children to Virginia when they reminisced about growing up in Mississippi.

My grandmother was known for her intense and unpredictable mood swings. When things weren't going as she expected, she took to her bed and waited out the gloom. I imagine that these incidents had little to do with the drama that played out in the home but rather swept her up like a bad headache. It could have been that she was upset because she was denied an invitation to an afternoon social at the home of one of her peers. Maybe she got overwhelmed by the shenanigans of the boys. She might have suffered from depression. Who knows. Mat would have been present and attuned to Mamaw's predispositions and undoubtedly was taken into her confidence.

Over on the Hall plantation, Simon found himself in love during those years. He and Sadie Gallion never married but they did produce a baby girl, Virginia, in 1932—one year after the Fields family moved to Greenfields. Little is known about their relationship except that Sadie was a "loose" woman who drank and partied so much that she was not able to care for Virginia. There was nothing to do but take his baby girl home to his mother, Leana, on the Hall plantation and that is where Virginia grew up. Charlie Lee Jr. was born two years earlier to Aunt Mat's daughter and her husband. Vivien was an unfit mother like Sadie, so his upbringing was left to Aunt Mat at Greenfields.

For the first four years in the new house, my grandparents carried out their parenting responsibilities and kept the cotton growing. Sometime in the fall of every year they travelled to New Orleans to the cotton exchange bearing samples of their valuable product. Thomas would ascertain the asking price per bale of his long staple cotton and presumably he'd find a buyer. Mamaw became a regular at the big department stores and food emporiums. She bought seasonal clothing for herself and the children as well as fine antiques that had to be shipped up river to the Delta. I imagine that during those trips, Mamaw was able to indulge her love of good food. She arranged for coastal delicacies to arrive in Anguilla at important times during the year.

On the night of November 9, 1935, the family feasted on fresh, raw oysters for dinner. Afterwards, the boys who were 13, 11 and 9, hustled into the back seat of Mamaw's black Buick LaSalle and were driven to a basketball game with a neighboring team. After they played, the family went home. Thomas wasn't feeling well—indigestion, he thought. He labored up the steps to his bedroom but made it only as far as the landing where he collapsed. Mat entered the back of the house about that time and sensed catastrophe. She did what she always did: corralled the children. I imagine her running bath water so she could get them clean and in their beds. I can just hear her saying, "Be quiet and do as I say or I'mon whupp you good."

Mamaw called the doctor in a panic. Thomas' diagnosis was "coronary thrombosis." He rested in his own bed that night while Mamaw made plans to take him the following day to Johns Hopkins in Baltimore. That trip didn't materialize nor did he make it to Mercy Hospital in Vicksburg, the closest medical facility to Anguilla. Thomas died during the night. A thick cloud of sadness and loss fell on Greenfields that night. Only when she had recovered enough to sense her new responsibilities did she speak with Mat, or maybe words were unnecessary. Mat would have been entrusted with the care of the children to a greater degree than ever before. Mamaw also pulled my father aside and said, "Son, you are now the head of this household." And thus began a long bereavement and a new order on the home front.

In the weeks and months following Thomas' death, Mat's role expanded even more to include essential care for the Fields children. Like Calpurnia in *To Kill a Mockingbird*, she held down the fort, operating out of the kitchen. Charlie Lee Jr. was five years old when my grandfather died. Mat had to count on him to take care of himself while she stepped in to help manage the Fields children because Mamaw's widowhood thrust her into a role as one of the first female planters in the Delta. And it was customary for black women to forsake their own motherhood roles in order to care for white children.

Aunt Mat in her uniform

Until June 2015, I knew very little about the atmosphere in Mamaw's home during such a difficult time, nor did I know how she drew on the strength of her kin to help her cope with her loss and the stress of a new role. It was then that I got a phone call from my father's cousin, Dr. Harold H. Hedges. I had only met him one time, in 1985 when Mamaw had fallen ill and was transported to St. Vincent Infirmary in Little Rock, Arkansas, where Harold was chief of staff. She was diagnosed with mesothelioma, a lethal type of lung cancer. Harold was her admitting physician in charge of Mamaw's evaluation and treatment. He kept her there after surgery, where in only a few days she died. The day I got word that my beloved grandmother, then 84, was seriously ill, I drove to Nashville, took a puddle-jumper to Little Rock and had my last visit with her. I entered the hospital room where she lay in a fetal position and when

I touched her arm, she opened her eyes, sat up in bed and announced to my aunt and other relatives, "Molly's here. Somebody get us a co-cola." She never let me down.

I was impressed with Harold the day I met him. His demeanor commanded respect yet he was gentle and kind. To hear from him again after thirty years was a happy experience. He called after his son had given him a copy of *Death in the Delta*.

Because so many family members objected to my writing the first book, Harold's open enthusiasm for it granted me a mixture of pride and relief.

This was my opportunity to speak with a living family member who grew up side by side with both my father and Charlie Lee Jr., Gregory's great grandfather. "They called me Dooneybug or Dooney for short," Harold told me. Then he went on to explain that after Thomas died, Harold's father picked up his young family and brought them to Anguilla, where he settled his wife and six months old Harold in one of the white clapboard houses built on either side of the main house at Greenfields. They worked it out that Harold's father would help run the gin and oversee the plantation until Mamaw's three boys got older. His mother, Jerry, would provide another parental presence about the house. For six years, Harold grew up in the midst of the Fields children aged 13, down to 6, along with Charlie Lee and another black boy, Sonny.

Twice Harold told me the story of his three-year-old birthday party. His parents gathered together a dozen or so children his age but they didn't plan to include Charlie Lee. Even at that tender age, Harold knew it wouldn't feel right to play games and eat cake without his best friend. He pitched a fit, maybe flung himself on the floor. Whatever he did, the rules were changed that day. Charlie Lee and Sonny were present for Dooney's birthday.

"Sonny" & Charlie Lee. at Harolds 3rd Birthday

Charlie Lee Jr (in the middle)—1937—Harold's third birthday

The two boys became inseparable. They walked all over Anguilla. Even though admonished not to go down certain streets, as long as Charlie Lee was by his side, Harold felt safe to go anywhere. They got over to Rolling Fork to the Joy Theater as often as they could to take in a western. The coloreds-only seating was in the balcony, so up Charlie Lee went, while Harold found an empty seat downstairs. They spent hours in the giant magnolia tree in Mamaw's front yard. And they rode double on horseback up and down the cotton rows and along the lane behind the big house. Harold didn't remember much about my grandmother except that she was respected by everyone on the home place. "She took good care of Aunt Mat and Jo," he said. "I am pretty sure 'Aunt Beck' must have helped my father financially through college as they had a close relationship." In a later email, Harold wrote to say that he'd "thought of an Aunt Beck story....I may have told you before about the day Beck literally saved my life......You may remember Beck's rose garden and gold fish pond by the left side of the house as you drove in. I was playing in the rose garden near the pond. Somehow fell in and was thrashing about. Beck was 'sitting' on the second floor bathroom commode looking out the window, saw me floundering, pulled up her drawers running down the stairs and out the door and pulled me from the pond. She reminded me of that episode annually."

One other memory stood out in his mind. Every day at noon, the wives and girlfriends of the field hands walked out between the rows of cotton to bring lunch to their men. No doubt there were certain old hardwood trees that offered a dense and wide canopy of leafy green protection from the oppressive heat, and there was space to stretch out. There, black men, women, and children rested, ate and sang songs. He said the women carried pails—old tamale cans—with cornbread and white beans. They ate from tin plates. Harold and Charlie Lee, though four years apart, often exchanged clothing and their friendship lasted until Harold's father moved the family to Arkansas so he could begin a career with International Harvester and Harold could start first grade.

Listening to him talk about those early years in Mississippi, I couldn't avoid smiling. He was so happy to have an opportunity to recall memories of Charlie Lee. At one point he chuckled and said, "I didn't know we were poor!" Evidently he was also too young to know that skin color could make a difference in how people were treated.

*Josephine, housekeeper for the Fields family,
standing before her shot-gun house*

FORTUNATELY FOR MY GRANDMOTHER, SHE'D MAIN-
tained close relations with her family of origin. Every
summer before he died, Thomas packed her and the
children along with Aunt Mat and sent them to the Riverby Inn in the Swannanoa, North Carolina, where the
climate was more temperate. The fourteen bedroom family
establishment run by Rebekah's parents was operated
much like a present day bed and breakfast. Not only did
her family welcome new and repeat visitors, but they also
experienced an influx of aunts, uncles and cousins. The
fresh, cool mountain air and loving embrace of the larger
family provided the perfect antidote to the long, slow, and
muggy days of the Delta especially after the loss of her
beloved mate.

My aunt wrote a description of a photograph of the family at the inn:

> *Riverby Inn is an old fashioned portrait of the Blanks Family arrayed before a two-story structure which, too big for home; too small for Hotel; dominates the Swannanoa Valley and is encased by the Blue Ridge Mountains. The white clapboard, green shuttered backdrop of early twentieth century, mid-American architecture gives depth to the group who are the focal point. The ancient mountain ridge frames the study in primary color which compliments the artist's conception of simple human relationship.*

Rebekah drove the long distance to North Carolina by herself with one stop over in Tennessee to break up the trip. About seven months after Thomas died, she left Anguilla to return once again to the bosom of her kin as she did most summers.

"Mrs. Fields, we were so distressed to hear about Mr. Fields. Our condolences. So sudden wasn't it? Such a young man." The manager of the Magnolia Hotel in Dixon, Tennessee, had hosted my grandmother on these annual jaunts to North Carolina.

Still dressing in black, eyes clouded, and biting her lower lip to stop its quiver, she replied, "Thank you Mr. Burrows. Yes, it was sudden. Tom was eighteen years older than me… but… well, Mamma was with me almost a month." She was struggling to carry on alone with the responsibility of the four young children, the farm and gin. But her sisters knew Rebekah's strength. One of them said to their mother,

"Why on earth would you worry about Beck? Even

though she is your baby, there's one woman who can more than take care of herself. She'll try to out-drive, out-maneuver every man on the highway. She knows all the roads like the back of her fat hand. She's the only woman I ever saw who can drive with a wad of chewing gum in her mouth; eat an apple; slap at the children and keep the car in the middle of the road, all at the same time."

This first trip back since Thomas died, Mamaw found the activity and hard work of helping her parents operate the Riverby a great elixir for her grief. She was convinced by her family to hang up her black dresses, to see that other people had endured losses as well and to open up to her pain. She confided, "You know Tom never even kissed me till after we were engaged. He respected me and told me so."

JUST AS REBEKAH WAS RECOVERING FROM GRIEF, SHE had to face the possibility of losing the plantation to Thomas' brothers. Fueled with anger and the intention to keep the land and the gin for her sons and daughter, she went to court and convinced the judge that though she was a widow with small children, she was up to the challenge. My grandmother had a spine of steel, and she would not succumb to the pressures society imposed on most women of her day. Even though Thomas had taught Rebekah the tools of the farm trade, she had a massive learning curve ahead of her. My father often said that she was never home. Running a plantation, a gin, a household would have been daunting for most anyone. But she had worked hard to maintain good relations with everyone who worked for her. She once said, "The greatest compliment I ever received was when I was settling up finances with one of my long-time workers. I showed him the books, told him what I figured he was owed and asked if there was anything he didn't understand. He replied, 'Ole Miss, whatever you say, I know is right.'"

Little did she know how profoundly her livelihood would be affected by the changes in farming that were underway. In 1936, the Rust Cotton Picker Company developed the first mechanical picker. It was demonstrated in Stoneville, Mississippi. Word of this major advancement in agribusiness would not have escaped my grandmother. But the Rust machine was not entirely successful. It wasn't until 1947 that the International Harvester Company bought out Rust and began mass production. The specter of mechanization had to be a hot topic at social events and around warming stoves in country stores and town diners. The farmers would be scratching their heads and surely their concerns would have trickled down to the black workers. By 1937, many farmers were buying their workers one-way tickets to Chicago and other northern destinations. Meanwhile, Rebekah maintained her charge of field hands and kept to the status quo.

She, like many wealthy planters in the South, eschewed the local public school system. In 1937, when my father was fourteen, she enrolled him in Riverside Academy in Gainesville, Georgia. Dad rarely, if ever, mentioned his experience at Riverside. I found his report cards in the back of his baby book. Mamaw kept almost all of them and they reveal an underachiever at first. He barely passed chemistry and failed his Spanish and Geometry classes. High marks in deportment indicate a well-behaved student. By April he was making "distinguished" if not "excellent" grades. Tom, Bill and Sis were also sent out of state to boarding schools. Rebekah's hold on her family was always tight but the responsibilities of childrearing passed from her to Aunt Mat to teachers in distant places.

Chapter 5

PTSD

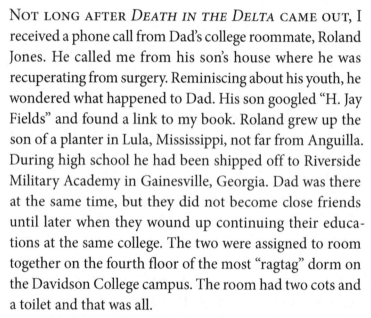

NOT LONG AFTER *DEATH IN THE DELTA* CAME OUT, I received a phone call from Dad's college roommate, Roland Jones. He called me from his son's house where he was recuperating from surgery. Reminiscing about his youth, he wondered what happened to Dad. His son googled "H. Jay Fields" and found a link to my book. Roland grew up the son of a planter in Lula, Mississippi, not far from Anguilla. During high school he had been shipped off to Riverside Military Academy in Gainesville, Georgia. Dad was there at the same time, but they did not become close friends until later when they wound up continuing their educations at the same college. The two were assigned to room together on the fourth floor of the most "ragtag" dorm on the Davidson College campus. The room had two cots and a toilet and that was all.

Roland remembered Davidson as a highly religious school and since he was not a Christian, he came under some pressure to convert. The Scots-Presbyterian influence was probably not lost on Dad. He was a firm believer his whole life and regularly attended church even after participating in the death of Simon.

It seemed important to Roland to set me straight about

Dad's character. He said that people of their generation knew they were racist and Dad was not like them. In other words, racism was an overt, conscious and verbalized mindset with no apologies. I heard these words but admittedly dismissed them. After all, in an all-white, all male institution in the 1930s, discrimination was probably hard to detect. At that time, planters and their children, especially in Mississippi, had an altogether different definition of the word "racist." For them, the caste system in place was justifiable, even normal. They'd grown up with it. Based on a very old notion that blacks were innately inferior, uneducable, of weak moral fiber, and good for nothing but hard labor, many if not most Mississippians were incapable of seeing the full humanity of blacks.

Handsome, broad shouldered and athletic, Dad reminded Roland of "L'il Abner" but unlike the iconic rascal, Dad was "intellectually inclined." He was an "All American Boy," intent on pursuing the opposite sex for "whatever they could provide." Dances were frequently held at the college, and since it was a boys-only school, girls came to town and stayed in approved housing. After a spring prom, Dad's date told Roland about the wonderful time she had had. Evidently she thought Dad was committed to her on some deep level. When Roland ran into her some time later, she said, "When you see Jay Fields, you spit in his eye for me."

Maybe Dad was a bit loose and free with the girls, but part of his character was sculpted in stone. When my grandmother laid the moniker "head of the family," on Dad's shoulders right after his father died, she loaded him with adult responsibility when he was only twelve. At fourteen, in 1934, he was shipped away from home to his first taste of independence, and he would have carried that weight with him.

Fallow land waiting for planting, December 2006

In 1939, while Dad was still at Davidson, the Second World War broke out. At the time, Simon was driving a tractor on a cotton farm while his seven-year-old daughter, Virginia, was growing up under his mother's watch. He would have known the tedious sun-up to sundown workdays out in the fields tilling up weeds that grew in endless rows of lush, green cotton plants. For his labor he would receive minimal payment proffered by an intractable boss. I'm not sure of his motivation, whether for better wages or perhaps a taste of a different kind of life, but Simon enlisted in the army in 1941 and joined the ranks of troops at Camp Shelby, near Hattiesburg, Mississippi. Military records indicate that Simon was a private, so he would have been under the supervision of a white officer. Where he was stationed is unknown. It wasn't until 1948, under the Truman administration, that

Molly Walling

desegregation of army troops took place.

If Simon had hoped for a reprieve from the segregated South in the military, he would not have found it. As author Stephen Ambrose pointed out, there were two wars going on at the same time, one at home and one within the ranks of the military. Nonetheless, Simon wore his olive uniform with pride as he fought alongside the enlisted. Based on what I now know, he had a strong commitment to serve his country at the risk of his own life.

In his junior year at Davidson, Dad felt the call to serve our country as well. He signed up for the Army Air Corp in Greenville, Mississippi, and trained to be a twin-engine pilot in Blytheville, Arkansas. Sitting in the cockpit of a B-17 bomber in WW II, his hands engaged with instruments, Dad experienced the happiest days of his life. That's what he told me years later. He loved serving his country during WW II, flying with the 12th and 15th forces out of Africa on fifty-two missions to places like Orte, Pisa, Naples, Pompeii, and Battapaglio, Italy; Augsburg, Austria; Athens, Greece; Sofia, Bulgari; and finally to the Benedictine monastery, Montecassino, as well as the Anzio Beachhead. While stationed in North Africa, Dad frequently corresponded with the black folks back home. One of his letters included this passage:

> *Mat, I know you and Tater will stay with Mama and look after her the best you can. I don't know what I would do if I didn't know that you older darkies on our place are looking out for everything. I wish it were so that there could be the relationship between white men and colored all over the world as it has been with my family and the faithful darkies we have*

kept for almost a hundred years. Colored people like yourself, John Parks, Zack Nick, Wesley Davis, old Sturdivant and some of our other colored families are as much a credit to your race as my Grandfather, Col. Fields; my father, Tom Fields and my Uncle, Grover Fields were to theirs. Rest assured yourself and hasten to assure your friends and neighbors that as long as the Fields blood beats in our veins we will devote ourselves to maintaining peace, comfort and propriety among those of you who have faithfully served us. To the others who have seen an opportunity in my father's death, my Mother's inexperience and my and my brothers' youth to make unfair gains for themselves, I have nothing but the toe of my boot but, for the faithful, hardworking Christian negro families, we have a home for as long as they live.

When I read this letter to Mat, I cringed at the subtle gratuity of expression that seeped into the context. Words like "faithful darkies," "credit to your race," and "propriety" void any true sense of gratitude or deep concern for well-being that Dad may have intended to convey. His threat ,"I have nothing but the toe of my boot" unmasks Dad's capacity for violence.

Combat missions exacted an horrendous toll on Dad's nerves. He saw several of his friends' planes plummet toward earth, spewing out black contrails behind them. He saw the horrors of war, and he had to have felt helpless at times. He was homesick for family and friends in Mississippi and the comforts of home. But nothing seemed to put out the fire of his passion for flying, his love of the drama of war. In the end, he was awarded the Distinguished Flying

Cross, the Air Medal with nine Oak Leaf Clusters, and the Commanding General's Citation for Valor.

In 1945, he was discharged to the army air base at Boca Raton, Florida. There he went through a period of decompression. He was in a persistent state of edginess, and he was emotionally numb, characteristics consistent with what we now call Post Traumatic Stress Disorder. According to the National Institute of Health's website: "When in danger, it's natural to feel afraid. This fear triggers many split-second changes in the body to prepare to defend against the danger and to avoid it." Dad told me that he couldn't talk about his time in the army with the officials in Boca Raton. Their solution was to give him sodium pentothal so that he could open up and share his experience. That was the prevailing remedy for PTSD then. If only he could have taken advantage of treatments available to veterans today like desensitization, talk therapy, anti-anxiety medication or anti-depressants, he might have avoided a dangerous situation in his future. He might have overcome his instantaneous "startle" response. Instead, those split-second triggers stayed lodged in his body and he compartmentalized his war experience, stuffing it in a closet deep in his mind. He would turn to this tactic for dealing with life's difficulties in 1946.

In the army, Dad and Simon would have discovered personal traits they didn't know they had such as courage under fire, pride of purpose, commitment to the homeland. Though they both came back at about the same time, only Dad was celebrated for his service in the army. There was a parade for returning white soldiers in Greenville. Wherever Dad went in Anguilla, he would have been slapped on the back and welcomed home. But Simon had a different experience. It was only in the black community that his service was acknowledged. Members of Simon's family told me that he was seen as a hero simply because he survived. He too may have had symptoms of PTSD.

When Simon returned he was expected to pick up where he left off, driving a tractor and working the fields. Dad's life took a different turn. First, he married my mother while still in Florida and then brought her to the Delta. She was a domineering woman like Rebekah, and like her mother-in-law, she meted out guilt and shame. Dad entered a relationship in which he could never "measure up" to Mom's expectations of a husband and provider, and he didn't.

It took very little time, once he returned, to figure out that he didn't like farming life. With my grandmother's financial help, he purchased the Sharky County newspaper, *The Deer Creek Pilot*. Scooping the news, writing editorials, interviewing people… those were the things he loved and did very well. Dad had the ability to make room for both sides of an argument. He was fair-minded. He was a "big picture" thinker.

Happy with his work, happy with his marriage and the new baby boy that was born to him and my mother in October 1946, Dad was in a good place at last. He didn't walk in his father's shoes, but he had two younger brothers more suited to agriculture, and they were working alongside my grandmother on the plantation.

The Pan Am Station, Anguilla, 2006

In 1946, our country was recovering from two world wars and the Great Depression. Dad and his siblings had developed a new approach to managing wealth. "Wars may come and go. Put your money into land."

Throughout the harvest season that Fall, tensions began to rise when black soldiers and other farm workers didn't show up for work but chose, instead, to spend their time in the coloreds-only barroom at the Pan Am station where they could buy bootleg alcohol. A petition was circulated in the town to shut the place down but community efforts were hamstrung because the local law enforcement officers were on the take. Blacks in general were chafing under a system that made their lives intolerable. Hopelessness, indifference and tamped down rage began to undermine black/ white relations even further. White bosses chose to press down harder on the backs of their charges. Meanwhile the specter of "big farming" was looming on the horizon. But perhaps more alarming was "… the quickening racial consciousness of blacks and white concern over the potential aggressiveness of returning black servicemen (that) led to escalating racial violence in the wake of the war…" (Cobb 212). James Cobb also writes "…that for a period of several months after the war black men were being killed at the rate of one per week" (213).

My father's brothers had a hard time accepting the changes coming to the Delta. One of them was in the early stages of addiction. Alcohol was his choice for dealing with stress. The other brother inherited the family illness of mood disorder. His mania manifested in anger. He was hard on the "darkies." Many years after this incident, in the late 60s, this brother became enraged at my grandmother. I heard several reasons for the argument that resulted in a violent outburst. The result was that Rebekah packed up and moved out of the Delta to Tennessee. She sought safety living near Dad's other brother in a house on the same street.

Years after discovering the family secret, I have had time to assimilate the various renditions of the story and to sort out the historic context of the times, the personalities of those involved and vagaries of the tellings. To the best of my ability, I have revisited the incident with a more nuanced view. On the night of December 12, 1946 Simon and his friend, David Jones, joined a group of drinkers at the Pan Am station late in the day. He was wearing his green army jacket that evening. My father, mother and the extended family had dinner at Rebekah's and gathered in the living room for cocktails. They must have been sharing their frustrations. That day, Josephine, the housekeeper had disappeared. She was purported to have run off looking for a man with a bottle. My grandmother was expecting company from Kentucky and wanted the house put in order for their visit. The strong possibility exists that she sent her sons to look for "Jo" at the juke joint in the Pan Am, located in the middle of town.

Dad, Bill and Tom arrived in town bearing arms. Everybody knew that it wasn't safe to go into the coloreds-only room, and it was an especially dangerous place to be on that particular night. They entered and demanded that everyone go home. The proprietor, sensing the tension in the air, left the premises so there was no one to stop them. When told to go home, Simon and David refused to leave. They said they wanted to finish their drinks. Someone started shooting, and Tom Fields took a bullet in his shoulder. Simon's friend David was shot and killed. When the place combusted into red hot anger, Simon took off for the door. He was gunned down in front of the building, refusing the brothers' demands that he, the "uppity nigger" wearing an army jacket, get down on all fours and crawl away. His death certificate indicated that he had a bullet hole penetrating his chest. That's how he died. The only mitigating circumstance is that Dad or one of his brothers found it impossible to differentiate whether or not they were in a mortal combat situation. In war, they had learned to dehumanize the enemy and when the showdown commenced, it would have been easy to fall back on indoctrination to that effect. Quick recourse to violence is one of the now well-understood signs of PTSD. But racism dehumanizes as well.

During the years I spent ferreting out the details of this story and writing them down, I held onto the belief that my father was at fault. He was, undeniably, complicit just by virtue of the fact that he was there, in the wrong place at the wrong time, with what he saw as good reason. Three state newspapers carried the story and reported that Dad was charged with manslaughter and would be heard before a grand jury in February of 1947. I didn't want to accept the fact that my father was capable of such criminal activity, that he could take another life, much less two, but in *Death of the Delta*, I set my father up as the villain because there didn't seem to be enough evidence to the contrary. As a writer committed to seeking the truth, I felt I had to conclude that he was guilty. The picture of Dad as murderer didn't square with the image of the man I carried in my heart. But he was the one charged, and there wasn't enough evidence to "convict" either Bill or Tom.

My father was a complicated individual. In the crucial moments when lives were shattered and lost, forces more powerful than the motivations and actions of a trio of men came together in a split second. As if stepping into the roles of players in a stage performance, the scripts had already been written. And though it is impossible to get inside the mind of any other person, whether a parent or not, I can surmise that Dad, the older brother, a good compliant son, determined to keep things in order so as to avoid disappointing his mother and being blamed for circumstances beyond his control, chose to press down the accelerator as he entered a hairpin curve. Instead of waiting to be blamed for what happened, he shouldered the responsibility instead. When the incident was over and the gun smoke had dissipated, he drove his brothers home, one of them wounded. Confronting his mother, he either told her the truth, or he didn't, but it came down to this: my father, capable of heroic action and unfailing love of family, took the blame for the deaths of Simon and David. I believe he did it to protect one of his younger brothers who was twenty years old and who stood to lose a foothold on the trajectory of his life. Dad knew that the prevailing climate was one not likely to find a white man guilty in a case against a black man. His mother, powerful and respected in the community, was capable of influencing the legal system, and my father, respected in the local writing community, had proven himself on the battlefield and was known to be a good and compliant son. She and the boys put their heads together that night and crafted a story of self-defense. She made sure they understood that the incident would be closeted and never spoken of. The strength of her demands kept the story undercover for sixty years.

In my readings over the years, the words of Dietrich Bonhoeffer, German theologian and anti-Nazi activist, support my best thinking about this story.

> The question of good must not be reduced to an examination of the motives or consequences of actions by applying to them some ready-made ethical yardstick.... For what right have we to stop short at the immediate motive and to regard this as the ultimate ethical phenomenon, refusing to take into account the fact that a 'good motive may spring from a very dark background of human consciousness and unconsciousness and that a 'good attitude' may often be the course of the worst of actions?

I have often thought about the effects of this incident on my mother, who was at home that night caring for a three-month-old baby. How could Dad jeopardize their future? After all, he might have been sent to prison. One aspect of Dad's character, was the innate tendency to want to smother flames as quickly as possible. In all probability, the firefighter in my father, in a moment of intense crisis, saw the shootings as a massive conflagration that trumped every other part of his life. I can't say I wouldn't have taken the blame in order to protect my siblings.

On the night of the shootings, word travelled to the Hall Plantation to Leana Toombs, Simon's mother and Virginia's grandmother. They reacted in horror and deadening sadness. This promising young man, their blood, had spent the previous five years fighting in the war, only to come home to gunfire on the main street of Anguilla. Virginia was fourteen years old and coming into womanhood. She would never get over the death of her father.

The all-white grand jury convened in February. They determined that there was insufficient evidence to send this case on to the courts for trial. Dad was free to live his life as if nothing seriously wrong had ever happened. White people in the social circle of my grandmother were kind enough or too afraid to even intimate knowledge of what happened. It was just "one of those unfortunate things" that should not be discussed.

My brother, Harris Jesse Fields, is the third and final male in our bloodline to bear this name. Jay is a good man, a thoughtful man, and a person who has supported this writing. Not long after I returned from California with the nuanced rendering of the story according to Simon's family, I relayed the details to Jay. His response:

Having slept on a first read of your sequel, I woke up
with a number of things that I wanted to mention.

First off, it's very disturbing to read Virginia's family's version of the shooting story. The whole thing about shooting Simon when he's down; the whole thing about making him do as they say, then shooting him when he doesn't (when he insists on his own dignity as a soldier and as a person) is "beyond the pale"—to use what I think is a Jewish phrase of complete and malignant injustice run amok. I honestly believe I know dad well enough to say that he did have a kind of moral compass (no matter how distorted by the Delta social system) and I honestly find it hard to imagine that he instigated something like that ~ wherever that leaves things. But regardless of who pulled the trigger (and it stands to reason the black fellows did not have revolvers), the only measure of mercy left is the forgiveness we carry for that particular night and the very, very stupid, very, very tragic actions that took place. ... I wonder how dad and Bill lived with it and whether there was any attempt in their lives to convert the tragedy into something of meaning. I sure hope so because I am extremely sorry for the event, and I can't imagine that it wasn't huge in the souls of dad and Bill in particular. In a very broad context, given the perfect storm theory, everybody involved could be considered a victim, but that is no excuse for the tragic loss of life.

The smoky mysterious figure in all this, for me, turns out to be my grandfather, Thomas. He is certainly a pivotal figure from many perspectives. If he'd been alive, it's doubtful that the event would have happened as it did in the first place but if it had, would he have come down on the side of justice and held the boys responsible and accountable?—kind of an interesting question. Further, there is his potential role as Simon's father. There's so much we don't know in there if that theory holds. For example would he have conceivably given a chunk of land to Simon not so much out of guilt but because he deeply cared for his mother and for him. We don't know and we're already wildly afield in the milieu of speculation. But I do think that Thomas is a largely unknown and unexplored character. What if he had a large heart and the romantic imagination of his eldest son, Jay. Dad seemed to be very taken with the man so, as a reader, I think I'd like to sniff out more about him. He remains at the crucible of the entire story.

It was a terrible night in 1946. But in the end, you'd kind of like to think both sides of the tragedy –the 'black' side and the 'white' side –worked their way through forgiveness and God's grace back to a place of contribution and meaning and hope. Certainly you are pointing to that on Virginia's family's side and your tracking down the story provides clarity, light and hope on the Fields side. It was so, so hurtful, that night, but between the lines of your book there is, these days, cause for celebration too. In a broad sense you're sitting on something of a miracle.

Jay

Chapter 6

MIGRATION

—◦≈◦—

After Charlie Lee Jr.'s arrival in California ahead of Virginia and their baby, he followed in his father's footsteps working as a freight checker for Southern Pacific. By 1947 the railroad was hiring black workers, though his father had been able to procure a job in 1944 because of his light skin color and blue eyes. Two years after Simon died, Virginia arrived by train with her baby, Charles. For the seventeen-year-old mother, the journey represented a fresh start, as she was leaving behind the tragedy. One year later, in 1949, Pat was born, followed by another son, Simon Bernard, who everyone called Nardi. Pat said on numerous occasions, "…when my parents were new to the west, life just swallowed them up." The pace was too fast for them, and they didn't know how to slow it down. Fortunately for the children, Charlie Lee Jr.'s step-mother, Mama Lilly, would turn out to be a stabilizing force. She kept a watchful eye on them when Virginia's and Charlie Lee's lives began to spin out of control in the new, more liberal social climate of California, where opportunities they never dreamed possible opened up for them. As with many immigrant blacks in the North and West, they encountered a different set of rules. In fact, there didn't seem to be any rules at all.

NOT LONG AFTER I VISITED THE FAMILY IN JULY 2013, Gregory was offered a job as a junior reporter for the ABC affiliate in Charleston, South Carolina. Pat celebrated his foray into the working world but with a strong measure of sadness that he would be leaving California. They corresponded almost daily via text messages. Pat had refused to enter the tech world except via her cell phone. Greg thought it was oddly funny that she could communicate with him via text messaging but couldn't email. As soon as he settled in the Deep South, he went through a training period followed by several months covering local news as a cub reporter. His relationship with Pat continued to nurture him over the miles. She encouraged him just as his mother did.

Pat was not privy to Gregory's Facebook entries but I was. Two of the messages he put out there for the world to read indicated a tinge of homesickness and disillusion about his job.

5/11/14

It's days like today .. where it really sucks being a young ambitious adult at the bottom of the ranks in your career .. you work every holiday .. you're away from family .. and it really brings your spirit down .. When I have kids they will definitely be aware of all the sacrifices I've made for them .. because as much as I love my career .. there is nothing more I'd rather be doing than spending quality time with the woman who gave me life LaToya Mills Dennis .. I love you so much and wish I could be there with you .. still .. from thousands of miles

away from Cali .. just wanted to send my love and tell you Happy Mother's Day.
Sincerely, Your oldest son.

6/25/14

It's amazing how when you say you're a reporter people think Hollywood .. glitz & glamour of being on tv .. But never think about what we go through to make air.. How hard it is to look a mother in her face with a camera & ask for an interview about the death of her son or covering a fire of someone who lost everything or busting that dirty politician .. Being a Journalist is more than the 2 minutes you see reporters on tv .. It's about the everyday lives we touch & making sure the story is told accurately.. While still maintaining your sanity because sometimes the weight of the story can get to you .. #LifeOfAJournalist

I gather from conversations with Pat that she gave Gregory plenty of advice before he left for South Carolina. She told him, "You make a mistake—you learn from it and move on." She cautioned him to do his best work and to be steadfast in his faith.

Though I had found Gregory to be positive in his thinking about race, his contention that we live in a post-racism era was deeply shaken in June 2013 after the trial of George Zimmerman who was charged with the murder of seventeen year old Trayvon Martin of Sanford, Florida. Zimmerman, a Latino, was carrying out his duties as neighborhood watch coordinator in a gated community. He shot Trayvon and later testified that he'd acted in self-defense.

Zimmerman was acquitted. In this widely publicized case, racial tensions flared. Many thought that Zimmerman was profiling Trayvon, acting on impulses that stemmed from the fact that his victim wore a hoodie and was black. The issue of inappropriate decisions on the part of the police department at the time of the shooting also fueled an angry public. Trayvon became the poster child for continued racial inequality in the new millennium.

During the days that immediately followed the trial, I read a Facebook entry from Gregory that surprised me. He was clearly incensed if not infuriated by the verdict and called for his "brothers" to take to the streets. I wondered how Gregory would fare working in the Old South where staunch conservatism grows like mold under aging houses in the soupy humidity of places like Charleston. But Gregory was deep into his training as a cub reporter so he would have to stifle strong emotional reactions in order to maintain his role of truth-seeker. I don't know how he reconciled himself to the Trayvon case. There were no further entries that elucidated his feelings, but I intended to discuss this with him in the near future.

In the ensuing months, my only contact with the California family was via phone or email. Pat and I talked frequently because I had many questions for her. Our relationship grew more and more comfortable. Gregory posted often on Facebook. He was keeping up with old friends and making new ones. On October 12, he posted:

A few years ago Richard Lee Robinson, DeJonique Garrison and I made a pact to see each other at the top… and as we climb the ladder and sometimes stumble and fall…It's so amazing to share in the success of my peers…my friends…Congrats Dej! You are gonna beast! #FindAWayOrMakeOne #SucceedOrDieTrying.

News Channel 4 in Charleston put Gregory to work after his training period reporting on cultural events, music, county fairs, and restaurants. Later, he covered stories related to zoning, medical issues, local ordinances. His reporting was lively and impassioned. No story seemed to receive less than his full attention.

I had no way of keeping up with Virginia so many miles away. My first visit began to fade in my memory so on November 4, Virginia's 81st birthday, I flew to Los Angeles again. Trips to California like this one gave me an opportunity to see my daughter who was living and working in the Silicon Valley near San Francisco. Pat picked me up at my hotel the next day with a clear agenda. She wanted to take me to the ocean and show me where she biked every day.

In 1968, when she was working as a clerk at Lucky's grocery, Grandma Lilly had given Pat a clunker to drive to work. The old Scirocco was a lemon and kept breaking down and that meant that she was late for work on numerous occasions. When she had saved enough money, she bought a bike. That seemed to solve the problem of transportation. Today, she rides her new Cannondale from twenty to upwards of thirty miles almost every day, often stopping beside the beach bike path at a favorite rock where she nestles into a crook in the stone to read in the sunshine.

We drove south and parked the car so we could walk to Manhattan Beach. Several miles of fast walking in the heat of the day took its toll on my jet-lagged body, but it afforded the perfect setting for Pat to open up about her family. In conversation, she tended to jump from subject to subject so I was often confused about characters in her story, especially Charlie Lee Sr. and Charlie Lee Jr. Their lives seemed to mirror each other's in the early years in L.A. Freight checkers by day, they benefitted from good wages and the efforts of the first union in the country established for and by blacks.

In *An Anthology of Respect: The Pullman Porters National Historic Registry,* Lyn Hughes writes, "During the peak of America's railroad industry, in the 1920's and '30s, there were an estimated 20,000 black Pullman porters, maids, and other railroad personnel, making this the largest category of African-American labor in the United States and Canada at that time."

I couldn't find access to the pay scale of porters or freight checkers, but it was substantial enough that Charlie Lee Sr. could accumulate some serious money. Once he did, he bought his property in Compton and two other homes. Years later he boasted to Pat, "See what I did? If I'd had an education, I would have owned the whole street."

Good wages were not the only benefit of working for the railroad. The union advocated for fairness and dignity. Hughes identifies five themes that emerged in the collection of data about railroad workers: "Self-pride, Belief in unity, Self-imposed standards of excellence, Dedication to the Union's cause and existence and Commitment to family" (9). Right here we have the seeds of promise that passed down from generation to generation. Descendants of black railroad workers became prominent members of society, working as scientists, jazz musicians, attorneys, political figures, doctors, lawyers and other professionals. Pat spent thirty-four years as a hard-working member of her family. She learned to be that way from her grandfather.

Charlie Lee's experience with the railroad would have allowed him access to the black newspaper, the *Chicago Defender,* which was in distribution in California via train. Most southern blacks migrating to far away ports of call brought with them in their physical appearance (rough, ill-fitting clothes) and in their dialects (slow and lyrical expressions), a clearly discernible "foreignness." *The Defender* took on the role of dispensing advice since it was at least in part responsible for luring black folks out of the racial climate of the South. The paper routinely posted lists of guidelines such as this:

> *Don't hang out the windows.*
> *Don't sit around in the yard and on the porch barefoot and unkempt.*
> *Don't wear handkerchiefs on your head.*
> *Don't allow children to beg on the streets.*
> *Don't appear on the street with old dust caps, dirty aprons and ragged clothes.*
> *Don't throw garbage in the backyard or alley or keep dirty front yards (Warmth 291).*

Perhaps the best advice offered to the newcomers was to get a job. That was not easy for many people, but good solid work had psychological benefits that helped ameliorate other obstacles they faced, including negative stereotypical profiling of southern blacks.

Life in Los Angeles must have felt heavenly to Charlie Lee when he first arrived. He could eat the fruit right off the trees. The climate was much more temperate than the one he left behind. The pace of life was lively. Out of the Jim Crow South, he would find purpose, not the deadening aimlessness that came from a system that promised no possibility of improving one's lot. He sought out and found fellow Mississippians, even cousins. But he'd left his family and friends behind and no matter how long he lived in L.A., he wouldn't experience another day when almost everyone he saw out his window would be someone he knew; a relative, a friend, an old lover.

During the early years of Virginia and Charlie Lee Jr.'s marriage, they needed the support of parents as they attempted to raise the three children. At one point, Virginia got a job working at a church. Charlie Lee rose early to pack a lunch for her, and he gave her bus money. Then he walked her to the bus stop and made sure she got on board, but she showed up at home again within a few hours. Pat said she was just "too lazy." I believe that Virginia's coping skills were severely challenged. She isolated herself in her bedroom. Clearly she was suffering for a number of reasons, not the least of which was the murder of her father. The children were put out in the hall, and the door was locked behind them. She spent her days reading—anything she could get her hands on—and writing poetry and short stories.

Mama Lilly had to step in and take care of Charles, Pat and Nardi. She took them to her house and made sure they went to the church across the street every Sunday. Pat recalled how Mama Lilly bathed, dressed and prepared them for church. She always put a bow in Pat's hair. Then she gave them each a nickel to put in the offering basket. "Don't keep this money and go to the store," she'd say. "That money is for the preacher." But one Sunday there came a knock on the front door after the service. Sure enough the pastor was there to confront the kids, and he asked why the basket was short one nickel. Pat laughed about this and told me that the three of them could make a nickel stretch a long way on the candy aisle at the grocery.

During this early period, Charlie Lee Sr. and Jr. had pocket change of their own, and they made use of it gambling about town. When they left home those evenings, both were clad in suits and hats. Pat said they were two "good-lookin" men and the women were all over them. Charlie Lee Jr. had a dalliance and this put a strain on his relationship with his father and with Virginia. The result was that Charlie Lee Sr. stopped going out on the town at night with his son. At home, Charlie Lee and Virginia fought. Their unhappiness and Charlie Lee's drinking began to affect the children. Virginia put her foot down and asked him to leave. He repented and begged Virginia to let him come back into their lives, but she refused him. Ultimately she asked for a divorce. As a result of indebtedness from the gambling, they lost the house. Virginia had to move the kids into a mission while she applied for housing and later they moved to a public housing development, Aliso Village. The family fell below the poverty line, and Virginia began to drink. She started taking pills to get out of bed in the morning and to help her fall asleep at night.

Pat recalls hearing her mother cry and say, "I want my Daddy." Charles and Nardi got sick of hearing it and told Pat it was her job to comfort their mother. It was all Virginia could do to get up and ready the kids for school. She had only enough money to make potted meat sandwiches with mayo. Occasionally they had bologna and that was considered a treat. On at least one occasion, after a visitor came to their home, the kids found money that had slipped out of a pocket and down into the cushions of the couch. They took the money across the street where they could buy stale donuts, two for a nickel. Then they secreted their sweets into lunch boxes for a treat later at school. In the ensuing years Pat, Charles and Nardi became very close, especially Pat and Nardi—thick as thieves, as the cliché goes. "We knew each other's thoughts. We were like twins."

The boys tried to make life easier for Virginia. When they were old enough to slip out of the house and make their way to Hollywood, they set up a shoeshine business and sold newspapers. Returning to the projects at night, they threw their money on Virginia's bed and said, "Here, Mom, this is for you. Look what we got."

After our walk along the shore Pat and I returned to the parked car. In the far distance was the Santa Monica pier, known then and now for its amusement park atmosphere. Pat's love of the beach began there. When Nardi and Charles could drive and own a car, they swept up Virginia and Pat for a trip to the shore. To be out on the beach after dark was a joyful experience. Pat said, "We had a good time." Small, slippery fish called grunion popped out of the ocean near the shore at dusk. California fishing laws prohibited fishing for grunion except during spawning season. When they landed on shore, preparing to bury their eggs, the kids were able to catch them and put them in a bucket to carry home where they'd be fried for supper. According to Pat, Virginia was a wonderful cook when she felt like it. She was especially appreciated for her made-from-scratch cakes.

Christmas time was hard for Virginia and her off-spring. There was little extra money for gifts and the special traditions of the season. But back in Anguilla, Aunt Mat gathered enough pecans from the trees on the lawn at Mr. Tom's and Miss Rebekah's house so that she could shell them and send a boxful to California with a gift of cash.

We decided to drive to Hermosa Beach, another trendy and expensive California seaside village like Manhattan Beach. We chose a restaurant with al fresco dining and ordered fish tacos. While we waited for our order, Pat began to talk about Nardi. At twenty-three, Nardi developed the bad habit of getting behind the wheel of his car while drinking. One night Pat had a horrible dream about him. She remembers its every detail. Nardi was driving too fast for his impaired reflexes to come to his defense. He ran off the road and into another vehicle. His car caught on fire and burned him to death. In the dream Pat was watching as the scene unfolded. She approached the car with fear and dread. Nardi "sat up—burnt to a crisp." The day after her nightmare, Pat talked with him and relayed the dream hoping he would put her fears to rest.

"Aw, Pat, that ain' gon happen to me."

Three months later the dream turned into reality. It was a crushing loss for Pat because she loved her brother intensely. For the next twelve months, she mourned his death, holed up in her house just as Virginia was now. "I wouldn't talk to nobody in the family for a solid year." It's impossible to know, but perhaps a loss so deep was enough to make Pat more compassionate towards her mother.

During our drive from Hermosa to Compton that afternoon, I decided to discuss my plans for a sequel to *Death in the Delta*. Some of the stories she was telling me were of such a personal nature that I felt hesitant to proceed with the writing. My editor had asked for a synopsis and chapter descriptions, so I asked Pat if I could read them to her. I explained that I wanted her to know exactly what the project would look like. Her blessing was essential if I was to go forward. I stuttered when explaining that characters in nonfiction need to be portrayed as they truly are. Would she find it offensive if I were to write about Virginia's frailties? She said, "The fact that my mother was an addict was just that—a fact. I understand."

As our long afternoon together was coming to a close, I wanted to spend some time with Virginia. I had questions for her but chose to let our conversation take its course. If and when she felt safe and comfortable enough, she would open up. As was usually the case, the TV blared in Virginia's bedroom. A segment on medicine had captured her attention. When I interrupted her viewing, she said that she'd always been fascinated with the human body, with health and wellness, illness and disease. Later I asked her what she would have become if she'd had the freedom to further her education. She said that she would love to have become a doctor—short of that, a nurse. She loved mysteries that involved physical evidence. When she was caught up in a story, she'd get books from the library to help her understand what was going on. There is no doubt in my mind that Virginia had the innate brainpower to accomplish the lengthy training to become a doctor.

After a long pause, I asked, "What's it been like for you to live in California?"

"I'd rather have stayed in Anguilla. There, everybody knew everybody else and cared about each other whether they were black or white." In light of what I had discovered about race relations in the South, I found her sentiments perplexing.

Email dated September 9, 2013

Hey! The new job is amazing. Still in training but I'll be going live a week from today.....Unfortunately my nana is not computer savvy at all. She couldn't use email to save her life lol...But she is good with text (how? I don't know). & remember if u need anything let me know. I am pretty busy but whatever it is you are doing I'm willing to help even if it's just getting in touch with my nana for u or helping set up a time best for you gals to chat. I pray everything works out!

Chapter 7

COVENANTS

∽∾∽

"Live in the moment and make it so beautiful that it will be worth remembering."

(FROM A PLAQUE ON THE
WALL IN PAT'S HOUSE)

AFTER OUR VISIT WITH VIRGINIA, PAT AND I RETURNED to her house. Originally, Charlie Lee Sr. bought the white bungalow, the house where Virginia lives, and later built the more modern rancher that belongs to Pat. At the time of his first purchase, in the late 1940s, the neighborhood was predominantly white and Italian. In my research, I discovered that white residents established restrictive covenants to keep blacks from moving into the Compton area, fearing that the value of their property would be compromised. Undoubtedly they pressured their neighbors not to sell to blacks. When unsuccessful at stopping the influx of immigrants of color, they moved out of the central city. This phenomenon, now known as "white flight," was happening in other parts of the country too, especially in cities like Chicago and New York, where millions of blacks from the South were migrating as well.

Molly Walling

The more time I spent with Simon's family, the more I came to care about them. Almost imperceptibly I felt a shift in my focus from the part of the *Death in the Delta* story that had to do with my father to a desire to know more about the hardships they had faced. I was captivated by the resiliency of African American's persistence in the face of ongoing obstacles.

Offenses against blacks desiring property ownership have been historically rampant and horribly unjust. Unfair advantage goes back to the beginning of slavery. Black labor in 1840 was responsible for the production of cotton, which made up 59% of exports leaving the U.S. at that time. Together with the work of blacks that contributed to the infrastructure of our country, prosperity as we know it in our society, especially the economy, was built on the backs of oppressed people who received little or no benefit from their labor. Unfair practices embedded in the culture in the days of tenant farming after Reconstruction continued unchecked until cemented in place by the federal government.

In his *Atlantic Magazine* article of May 21, 2014, "The Case for Reparations," Ta-Nehisi Coates explores the issue of racist housing policies.

Like the Home Owners' Loan Corporation (which bilked Chicago's black homeowners out of rightful ownership and millions of dollars) the Federal Housing Administration initially insisted on restrictive covenants, which helped bar blacks and other ethnic undesirables from receiving federally backed home loans. By the 1940s, Chicago led the nation in the use of these restrictive covenants, and about half of all residential neighborhoods in the city were effectively off-limits to blacks.

We know that after their marriage in Mississippi, Charlie Lee and Mama Lilly went to Chicago when they left the Delta. Once there, they determined and were advised that it was best to head west. We don't know if Charlie Lee caught wind of prevailing practices in Chicago, but we do know that similar resistance was in place once he landed in Los Angeles.

At first, Charlie Lee bought a house on Century Boulevard in an area where many blacks were settling. As luck would have it, when the city decided to build the I-105 freeway, he was bought out, so he had enough money to purchase the walled acre lot with a white bungalow. Pat said, "He had no problem buying the house but before long, other blacks moved in and things began to deteriorate." As Ta-Nehisi points out, the fear of loss of property value that underscored the impetus for white flight became a self-fulfilling prophecy. Individuals like Charlie Lee moved into Compton only to watch as fellow blacks who couldn't get housing loans or other financial support had to let home maintenance become a lesser priority than basic survival needs.

But Charlie Lee Sr. was proud of his property and cared for it well. Pat pointed out a row of pine trees along the street. Because her grandfather had planted, pruned and shaped the trees, Pat has done the same. We walked into the backyard and were greeted by a yappy, over-amped Chihuahua-mix named Nardi, after Pat's brother. Clearly, he had a firm hold on Pat's heart. She proudly showed me the flowers she was growing, the trees she was caring for—lemon, lime and avocado, and the scraggly grass that wouldn't take hold and grow. Though there is already a third, separate building the size of a two- car garage, Pat is having a sun shed built so she can enjoy relaxing in her garden. Troubled by the evidence of a gopher invasion, she told me she's constantly battling the critters by pouring poison down their holes. Her well-tended oasis is subject to neglected neighboring properties.

"Come with me," she said while she placed a ladder against her cinder block wall and motioned for me to look over into the next yard. The varmints were coming from there. I saw old junky cars, trash, and chickens running wild. Then she carried the ladder across to the wall on the other side.

"Climb up, Molly." There a large tarp was suspended between trees to make a tent. Outside of it were cooking utensils. Pat said her Mexican neighbor was letting someone live there on his property. "He's growing marijuana over there."

Over the years the neighborhood has seen good days and bad. When Pat reached high school age, she settled there with her father so she could attend Compton high school, considered one of the better schools in the district at that time. Later, the gangs moved in and painted up the whole area with graffiti. But Pat swears, "It's much better here now." She calls the cops routinely to report loud music and because of her persistence, they now fine troublemakers. Her neighbors, mostly Latino, look out for her, and she does the same for them.

"I try to keep a good rapport with them but there are rodents and possums living in the back yards of many homes." One recent summer, Nardi escaped and ran around the street before Pat could catch him and bring him home. Several days later, she noticed a flea infestation inside her house. "It started with those big dogs on the street and spread all over. Now I have to keep Nardi penned up all the time." She gives him hell if he tries to get past her and out the door. "It took forever to get rid of those fleas."

Later I was able to piece together the problem with infestation and large, ominous dogs as they relate to the Latino community. Pat said that Mexicans, associated with drug cartels bought big lots. The dogs were for protection against druggies, cops and other intruders. This is Pat's understanding and may be only partly true.

I asked Pat why her grandfather gave the house to her instead of to her brothers, Charles and Bernard. She reminded me that when Virginia and Charlie Lee Jr. were struggling with their marriage and Virginia was slowly sinking into the quicksand of alcohol and drug abuse, she and her brothers had to be cared for by their grandparents. Charlie Lee Sr. and Mama Lilly stepped in and started raising them, but Pat was the favorite child. The feeling was mutual. After school every day she went home to do whatever she could for her grandparents. But when she was seventeen, she became pregnant and had her first child. She married and soon there was a second child. When it became necessary for Pat to work to help support her family, her grandfather got her a job at Lucky's Grocery and while she worked, he and Mama Lilly took care of the next generation. His strong work ethic was not lost on his granddaughter and he admired that about her. As time went on, Pat's own marriage began to disintegrate. She married again and this time, she and her new husband and their combined families moved into an apartment.

One day while visiting in Compton, Pat sat down at the kitchen table with Charlie Lee. He said, "Pat, your brothers have houses. They don't need a house. I want you to get this one. You work so hard to pay the rent. Bring your family here. This is where I want you to live." Pat's childhood experience mimicked the generation before. Just as Simon's daughter, Virginia, was raised by her grandmother and Charlie Lee Jr. was raised by Aunt Mat, Pat had the good fortune to have loving grandparents as well. Undoubtedly, these grandparents benefitted from the joy of transmitting values and family traditions.

When I thought about the history of slavery and the millions of Africans transported to the U.S. on "Guineamen" boats, for the sole purpose of providing labor on the growing number of large plantations, I remember that the destitute, preliterate individuals destined for servitude 'were stripped of all they knew and brought into a white, patriarchal society in which they faced a Sisyphean climb to adjust and prosper in a culture they didn't even want to be a part of. Negro family structure emerged as a result of the fact that blacks could depend only on each other for essential needs. Because the men in these families were often displaced— sold or moved away from loved ones—the role of black women as providers and sustainers of the family resulted in what E. Franklin Frazier termed a matriarchate. In time, the grandmother figure emerged as vital and predominant. She alone became "the repository of the accumulated lore and superstition of the slaves and was on hand at the birth of black children as well as white. She took under her care the orphaned and abandoned children" (Frazier 114). These oldest members of the family embodied quiet dignity and grace as well as power.

Because early African Americans had no recourse other than to submit to the dire circumstances in which they found themselves, religion and specifically prayer became increasingly important. In this story, it is clear that Aunt Mat, who took responsibility for raising Charlie Lee Jr. and Leana, who took Virginia under her wing, left their families with legacies of tender care, personal strength and deep, abiding faith. No doubt Mama Lilly, along with Charlie Lee Sr., provided the same consistent parenting for Pat, Bernard and Charles. Today, Pat has assumed the position of family head even though her mother, Virginia, is still alive.

Pat recalled with great pleasure one Christmas experience growing up with Charlie Lee Sr. and Mama Lilly. On Christmas Eve they baked cookies for Santa and then the children were tucked in for the night. Bernard was stealthy, and when he cracked the bedroom door open to spy on Santa, he saw Charlie and Lilly sitting at the kitchen table having coffee and munching on the chocolate cookies. The kids had a good laugh and still tell each other that story.

While I was in California getting to know his family, Gregory was working hard to make connections and prove himself as a reporter. I read his Facebook entries with interest and a smile. He was missing his California roots but his faith was carrying him into a hopeful future.

Problems Cali ppl have when they leave LA .. No Roscoes ..No In &Out .. No Taco Trucks .. No Ramonas .. No Bills Taco .. No Late night two tacos for a dollar @ jack & the Box & for all my IE ppl No Bakers! & for all my bay area ppl No Nation Burgers .. Huh leavin Cali is leavin more than just sunny weather the beach & beautiful women .. Its leaving everything i know isn't good for my health but good for my taste buds! Huh #MissingHome

And

I'm so used to being a broke college student .. That sometimes I forget when the news is talking about white collar corporate america...They're now talkin bout me too! #PraiseBreak on the realization I'm not struggling in college anymore & my studies/degree paid off #OnMyWayToMyDestiny #Philippians3:14

When I found out that Gregory was the first person in his family to get a college education and that he had completed a master's program at the University of California Berkeley with honors, I wondered who or what in his youth had influenced him. Later I would learn the sources of his motivation, but at this time I was aware of the stark reality that many young black males ended up incarcerated for various infractions mostly stemming from drug abuse. Though Gregory had two step-brothers, whom he considered to be full-blood kin, serving out sentences in jail, he also had a brother, Davante, and a younger sister, Megan, who shared the same father with him. Latoya was their mother.

Why had Gregory chosen a healthier, less destructive path than his step-brothers? What had kept him focused? Why hadn't he become disillusioned when he met with obstacles along the way? Why hadn't he succumbed to dependence on addictive substances? Why hadn't he fathered a child out of wedlock or become an absentee father? I looked for answers in Michele Alexander's book, *The New Jim Crow: Mass Incarceration in the Age of Color-blindness*.

...America is still not an egalitarian democracy. An extraordinary percentage of black men in the United States are legally barred from voting today, just as they have been throughout most of American History. They are subject to legalized discrimination in employment, housing, education, public benefits, and jury service, just as their parents, grandparents, and great-grandparents once were (Introduction).

When I think about what it would be like to be oppressed on so many fronts, especially in education and employment opportunities, I start to understand how the deadening effects would become encrypted on a person's soul to the extent that he or she might self-medicate so as to make it from one day to the next. Look at Virginia,

Alexander points out that the incarceration rate in the U.S. is six to ten times that of any other industrialized nation. She quotes staggering statistics.

In two short decades, between 1980 and 2000, the number of people incarcerated in our nation's prisons and jails soared from roughly 300,000 to more than 2 million. By the end of 2007, more than 7 million Americans—or one in every 31 adults—were behind bars, on probation, or on parole (18).

Because the percentages of racial minorities is extraordinarily high, she suggests that our society is intent on putting blacks back in their place and the "War on Drugs" is how we justify it. The criminal justice system has become an institution determined to maintain the racial castes that emerged with slavery. It is responsible for the demise of many black families due to the displacement of father figures. Not only does white society perpetuate the notion that blacks are somehow inferior, as manifest in the subtle practices of institutional racism, but in the current political climate, it takes no responsibility for the inequalities and places the blame for all kinds of sociological ills on people of color.

A quick search of the South Carolina Department of Corrections website produced a profile for inmates. Charleston, where Gregory was reporting, is the second largest city in the state but fourth in committing criminals. The information, dated June of 2013, provides telling numbers. Of the total population in correctional facilities, 64% are black, 20,000+ are male as opposed to 1300 female. Only 30% of the males are listed as married, while 46% of the women have spouses. Not surprising is the fact that the percentages of offenses for dangerous drugs and homicides are the same.

In Gregory's news broadcasts on Facebook, I noticed that he frequently mentioned the steady stream of murders in his city. Covering those stories was difficult.

Mayor Summey: there are too many illegal guns floating around the Lowcountry @ABCNews4

Elder James Johnson: the number of women dying at the hands of gun violence is on the rise in Lowcountry @ABCNews4

Tonight @ABCNews4 hear what a group of local activists & law makers say needs to be done to stop violence #chsnews

WHEN THE TIME CAME FOR ME TO LEAVE L.A. AND head for North Carolina, Pat gifted me with one more story, this time about her own travail. It started when she was at work at Lucky's grocery. True to her extroverted personality, Pat loved her job because she could interact with the public every day. She tried to brighten the moments at hand for her customers by getting to know them and caring about their lives. One day while helping out in the warehouse, a forklift pinned her to a stack of pallets. She told me it hurt like hell and caused her to have severe back pain. Finances in the family were such that she couldn't afford to miss a day at work. She loaded up on pain meds and soldiered on until her body insisted that she see a doctor.

During her exam, the doctor ordered x-rays of Pat's spine. The scans showed evidence of severe nerve damage. He asked her if she'd suffered any injuries at work. When she recounted her run-in with the forklift, he told her that she had a disabilities claim. In the end it took thirteen years to settle her workman's comp case. The money she received was, I'm guessing, substantial. It came to be a very important ally.

In the early 1990s, Pat married for the third time. When she met her husband, he presented as the perfect match, attentive and adoring. But, according to Pat, shortly after their vows were official, he pulled a "bait and switch" on her. He moved into her house on 130th Street and immediately began to berate her and abuse her verbally and emotionally. Their marriage lasted twenty years. During that time he took advantage of Pat's generosity and contributed less and less to maintenance of family life. Pat continued to work every day and when she decided she had had enough abuse, she told him to move out. He refused, claiming ownership in her house. For reasons unknown to me, Pat felt she had to buy her way out of the relationship. As soon as the disabilities check arrived, she had the means to write him a check and send him on his way.

That was in 2013. Since then Pat has flourished. Her back problems have abated so she is able to ride her bike again. Her fit and toned body is strong evidence of good physical conditioning. At home, she has painted the rooms in her house vibrant, pastel colors to create an atmosphere that suits her California lifestyle. Old family pieces have been restored, family photographs reframed, the kitchen remodeled so that she can prepare her favorite foods. On my first visit, she proudly displayed her collection of extra virgin olive oils and the many fruits and vegetables in her refrigerator. She held up a large bag of avocados and told me that her health could not be better. Perhaps she is most proud of the benefits she sees in her mother as a result of her cooking.

Chapter 8

THE POET

In the spring of 2014, I hit a wall when I tried to go deeper into the Virginia Toombs story. The pieces wouldn't fit together because of deep holes in my understanding. So many characters inhabited my mind. The timeline was underdeveloped in places. Why was I still pursing it? I felt that Gregory's perspective would be helpful so I sent him an invitation to drive from Charleston to the mountains of Western North Carolina. At first he seemed enthusiastic, and we planned for him to visit on his days off in the early weeks of June. But as the time drew near, he waffled and stopped communicating with me. To accommodate his busy work life, I offered to make the five hour drive to Charleston. He responded that he had to be in Charlotte in a week and I could get to Charlotte in half the time. We could meet and talk then.

I thought of all kinds of reasons for him to put me off. By July, I had plans to go to California to celebrate my daughter's birthday in Carmel in late August. A phone call to Pat let me know that she would be available if I wanted to fly down to L.A. before departing for home. Again I considered reaching out to Gregory. With his input, I might ferret out some details that I could then explore with Pat and Virginia. I've never been one to give up easily but the thought of being a nuisance wasn't comfortable. Late in July I screwed up my courage and sent Gregory an email with a few simple questions. Since he was such a high achiever and so hardworking, he might respond to this means of communicating, and it might not stress him out as much. I waited out the weeks until August but got no response.

When I discussed this problem with a fellow writer who had been reading along as I wrote, he said that realistically, a twenty-five year old starting a new career in a city far from home would be consumed with the responsibilities he faced. And he felt that perhaps, when Gregory first discovered *Death in the Delta* he became fascinated by his family's story, but now the glow had faded. I was discouraged but prepared to accept this dilemma for what it was.

Los Angeles, August 31, 2014. I flew into LAX in time to settle in my hotel by lunchtime. Pat's 65th birthday had come and gone the same day as my daughter's, August 28th. Our plan was to have a celebratory lunch together and then visit Virginia. She wanted to straighten Virginia's room and prepare her for company. We settled on a Cal/Mex restaurant and talked deep into the afternoon.

The first item I wanted to explore with Pat was the timing of both Charlie Lees' deaths. I had assumed that Charlie Lee Jr. was preceded in death by his father, but that was not the case. In the early 1980s, when Pat was between the ages of thirty-five and forty, her father, Virginia's husband, was stricken with cancer. During the final stages, when he was hospitalized, Pat visited him every day. He begged her to get the doctors to unplug him. He thought they were experimenting on his body, so any sense of dignity was compromised. Finally Pat agreed. Before he died he said, "You know I love you. I was never able to express it because of my grandmother." He was referring to Aunt Mat, who raised him in Mississippi, and to her inability to show affection and love. Pat told me that her father had always watched out for her and made sure that she was okay.

She said, "After we buried him...that night...I was in bed and felt something over me. I was afraid someone had gotten in the house. But it was 'warm energy,' a body or something. I felt the weight of it. And then, my daddy kissed me on the cheek. I felt it and knew that it was him."

At the time of her ex-husband's death, Virginia had moved out of Aliso Village and into an apartment. When I pressed Pat for more details about her parents' relationship she surprised me with a new revelation and a wonderful story.

Heretofore, Pat had painted a picture of marital bliss when Virginia and Charlie were first married and living in a house given to them by Charlie Lee Sr. Her childhood recollection of them was colorful. Charlie Lee came home every day and busied himself in the yard, mowing and caring for the exterior of the house. Meanwhile, Virginia was inside, cooking for the family. Pat remembers her mother wearing pretty dresses with petticoats and smart shoes. It was a happy time for the couple and their three children.

But after Charlie Lee became involved in gambling and drinking, he came home after nights out on the town and they argued. The tension in the house grew thicker as he was pursued by and pursued other women. Prior to this conversation Pat had not revealed to me that Virginia was unfaithful as well. One of Charlie Lee's cousins from Mississippi, Harry Washington, a schoolmate, became enamored of her and she gave birth to his child, Van. And to my amazement, there was a fifth child, Tiny, born during that time to yet another father. Hope for Charlie Lee and Virginia's relationship began to fade. Virginia foresaw the train wreck of her marriage and asked Charlie Lee for a divorce. He begged Virginia to reconcile, but she would not relent.

After that, when Charlie Lee came by to see his children, Virginia locked them in the house and refused to allow him in or to let the children see their father. Eventually, Charlie Lee elicited the help of his father. The two of them would drive to Virginia's house only to be met with resistance, but Charles, Nardi and Pat caught on to the game their parents were playing. They escaped through the back door, ran around to the front yard and into the arms of their father and grandfather.

Charlie Lee would say, "Yep, those are Anderson hands … hard-working hands. Yes, those are Anderson legs." Pat smiled when she told me this. Her adoration of her father was immense.

"To me, we had a good life," Pat said. "I felt love in the house." Even during the hard times when family funds dried up, forcing Virginia to move into public housing, Pat never questioned that her mother loved her.

"One time she fed us flour and said, 'pretend it's chicken.'" The children did just as they were told. "We never felt deprived."

When Pat, Nardi and Charles were old enough to leave Virginia's nest, they did. That left Virginia alone with the dregs of a painful childhood resurfacing and taking her down. To cope, she drank, took drugs and wasted away. Her environment reflected her inner world. Filth collected in the kitchen and everywhere else. On more than one occasion, she attempted to end her life. By then Pat had established a work life that was fulfilling and putting food on the table. At one point she held down two jobs. In addition to clerking at Lucky's grocery, she spent her two days off each week doing yard work for a retired teacher, who paid her well and appreciated her work. A strong friendship grew between the two women.

I asked Pat how she was able to manage after the forklift accident at Lucky's. She said that when she was injured, she fell to the ground seeing stars. Someone said, "Oh Pat, we need you. Go lie down. We need you." Because of her loyalty to the store and its other employees, she soldiered on, pain and all. Then, some years later, while running in a marathon, "the pain came out of nowhere." Pat's doctor gave her medication but it only masked the symptoms. Finally he said, "You keep coming down here to see me for the same problem. Get a workman's comp doctor."

I couldn't imagine Pat in any condition other than robust health. She was the picture of fitness and youth. "What have you done to get your health back?" I asked.

"I listen to my body and I'm careful to do what feels good and not do what feels bad."

In 1993, when Pat was 45, Charlie Lee Sr. died. For several years he had campaigned to have Pat move out of her apartment and into his house. Finally she consented and began to move her belongings to 130th Street little by little. Three days before she completed the move, when Charlie Lee was going to the eye doctor, he had a massive stroke at the medical facility and never recovered.

Compton, late afternoon, August 31.

Because of heavy Labor Day traffic, the drive from the restaurant to Virginia's was slow and tedious. It seemed as if the whole city of L.A. was heading for the beach.

When we got to 130th Street, Virginia was sitting up in bed, watching television. It was murderously hot in her little house. There was no fan in her room and the windows were open only slightly, but the weather was of no concern to Virginia, who wore a long- sleeved baby-blue flannel gown and appeared to be comfortable.

The first thing I noticed was how frail Virginia looked. Clearly she had lost between twenty and thirty pounds since my visit the previous November. Pat was worried about her weight loss too. As I sat on the stool beside her bed, sweat rolled down my face and neck and I found it almost impossible to think, much less ask the important questions I had for her.

"How you been?" Virginia asked.

"I'm well, thank you, but I lost my mother this spring. It's been hard to adjust, but I'm recovering."

"Oh… I'm sorry," she said. "When a person dies, there is a void that can't be filled—a void in the heart."

"Yes. And you have known that for most of your life, haven't you." I was touched by the emotional warmth Virginia could project at 81. But the actual heat in her bedroom was overwhelming and even she seemed too tired to continue to talk. I left her with a promise that I would ask Pat to lock all of the doors. She told me not to forget.

While I was talking with Virginia, Pat was scrambling through the attic of her house trying to uncover a box in which she had stowed her mother's writing. I'd asked if she thought Virginia would mind if I read her poetry, if there were any old photographs that I might copy. For the next two hours, Pat and I worked side by side in her kitchen, going through an old briefcase that had belonged to Virginia. In it were spiral notebooks full of homework assignments. At one time, she had studied to be a secretary. On odd pages were handwritten verses. I read them out loud to Pat, who listened intently but at least at first, didn't seem to be emotionally invested in her mother's work. I began to suspect that when Virginia was reading or writing or studying, she was unavailable to her children. Her physical presence was enough to make them feel secure, but her need for solitude created emotional distance. She was often out of reach to them.

Late in the afternoon, the sun was heading toward the horizon. The overhead lamp created a soft glow around Pat and me. I found myself transported as I read Virginia's lovely poetry. Her words were carefully chosen, written in free verse with no particular pattern evident. They did not rhyme. They were not sing-song. They expressed a deep connection to the divine. She wrote in praise of the glory of the universe. There were thoughts on how to overcome depression—"just take a step, just take a step." I noticed as I read that Pat, who runs through her days lickety-split, was slowing down and imbibing the essence of her mother's words. Our connection seemed so real to me in the intimacy of that shared time.

I found a journal entry written when Virginia was pregnant with her fourth child. She referred to him as Baby Van and wrote lovingly about her fetus and how happy she was to discover that she was carrying him. Early on in her pregnancy, she began to have problems and her doctor told her she would need surgery. She fought him because she didn't want to lose her baby on the operating table, and she put it off for a week until he convinced her that the baby would die if she didn't take care of herself. The surgery was successful. She carried Van beyond the forty-week mark and he was okay.

In another journal entry, Virginia mentioned Pat by name, recalling a time when her beautiful daughter stood before her. As I read, Pat became quiet and thoughtful.

I said, "Pat, it is so clear to me that Virginia loves you— all of you—so much. And you have to appreciate her contemplative nature. She was able to nurture her spiritual life even though she suffered from depression. I am beginning to see how big-hearted your mother is and always has been." Then Pat stopped shuffling through papers, sat down on a stool and leaned in.

At that moment, perhaps for the first time, I saw how our lives had unfolded in parallel. I wished that someone who knew my own mother had taken me aside before her death so as to recall her life, her gifts, her complexity. She too was distant at times and unavailable. As a child I thought I was at fault, that some part of me was unlovable. Now that she is gone, I know differently.

Deep in the pile of papers I uncovered an open envelope addressed to Virginia Anderson. It was postmarked Feb. 15, 1972 and had been sent out by the Institute of Mental Physics. At that time, Pat was twenty-three years old. A quick google search provided the following information:

"the (Institute's) retreat center is the oldest and largest retreat center in the Western United States; a unique architectural landmark on a 420 acre sacred site. As a non-profit 5011(c)(3), our mission is 'Promoting the physical, mental and spiritual well-being of mankind.'"

Early in our acquaintance, Pat told me that Virginia had been "into metaphysics." I wasn't certain how she was using those words.

Further reading revealed that the institute was founded by Edwin John Dingle, who was fascinated by all things Eastern and had been one of the first Westerners to enter Tibet. He stayed there studying and practicing the prevailing Buddhist traditions until he felt prepared to return to the states, in 1927, where he began to disseminate his teachings –the ancient wisdom of the Brahma Vidya, now known as "mental physics". Here is where I connected the dots that told me so much about Virginia. "Mental physics is an experiential method of self-realization that teaches the oneness of life embodied in all substance, energy and thought."

To me this sounded a lot like quantum physics. The tenets of her philosophy are basic to all religions. To my way of thinking, Virginia was ahead of her time.

My experience of Virginia had not in any way referenced her belief system. She was too private to open that door with me or probably anyone else. Half her lifetime ago, she was doing the kind of deep inner work that would have led her toward self-discovery and understanding. At some point, the scars that came with the loss of her father were triggered and leeched out pain and sadness to the extent that she couldn't bear it. Her reliance on drugs and alcohol intensified. With compromised inner resources, she went to the bridge where she planned to end her life. If Virginia had been born white, she could have availed herself of psychological help. Her tendency toward self-destruction would have been recognized as mental illness.

That day, Pat was at Lucky's Grocery when she received a phone call from Virginia's neighbor and best friend, Valerie, who told Pat that her ex-Marine brother had been trailing Virginia. She had been drinking and acting out. He tried to control her, but she left home with Simon's portrait and headed for the tallest bridge near her apartment. When he failed to talk her down, he called the police. Virginia was saved and taken to the hospital. Soon after, Pat helped her move into the white house, 130th Street, Compton. She carries the horror of that day in her heart.

Chapter 9

HEAT

_____ ⌾⌾⌾ _____

January 18, 2015

WINTERTIME IN THESE BLUE RIDGE MOUNTAINS WHERE
I live can be dreary. Constant use of forced heat causes
everything in my house to dry out, including me. Some days
the wind chill factor makes me wish I didn't have to walk
my energetic white lab, Toby. On especially cold mornings,
I almost consider withholding food and water so he won't
need to go out. After the holidays with family and friends,
the loneliness that comes with living solo drains the glow
out of my life. To remedy the malaise, I will usually make
a run down to the coast for several days. There, off season,
the beach yields itself to long walks, and the restorative
salty air revives me.

Folly Beach is just about my favorite stretch of shoreline
along the Carolinas. I phoned the inn on the waterfront,
where I usually stay, and made a reservation with two
thoughts in mind: first, relax. Next, try to see Gregory, since
Folly is right next to Charleston where he now lives and
works. Maybe he would agree to a visit on his turf. He did.

The day before I left, I stood in my study shaking my
head at the mounds of newspaper and magazine clippings

that amassed on my desk, seemingly overnight. In the previous six months three highly publicized racial incidents had occurred, and taken together with the Trayvon Martin case, seemed to be shaking up a society that had become complacent in what many deemed a "post racism" culture. Clearly, the time had come for us all to wake up to the reality that the wounds of the past were re-opening. Esteemed black historian John Hope Franklin wrote in his autobiography that there "…was never a moment in any contact I had with white people that I was not reminded that society as a whole had sentenced me to abject humiliation for the sole reason that I was not white."

July 17, 2014

Staten Island, New York. Eric Garner died from a chokehold administered by police.

August 9, 2014

Ferguson, Missouri. Eighteen year old Michael Brown was shot twelve times by Officer Darren Wilson when there was no apparent threat.

November 22, 2014

Cleveland, Ohio. Twelve-year-old, Tamir Rice died after a police officer mistook his toy gun for the real thing.

In all three incidents, the justice system came down on the side of the police officer. This kind of gratuitous violence combusted into massive civil unrest. In Ferguson, Missouri, riots, looting and destruction of property resulted in National Guard intervention. People of all colors took to the streets to march in protest when the officer in charge was not indicted. Unlike the early days of the Civil Rights Movement when news traveled at a slower pace, the internet enables a message to reach a critical mass with such speed that protesters can assemble in a matter of hours. On college campuses, student activities mobilized quickly; students from four colleges and institutions in and near my hometown of Asheville made multiple trips to Ferguson. They were a small contingency of the broad coalition who seemed to be shouting at all of us to register their refusal to tolerate any more injustice.

For me, it seemed as if the racial pulse rate of our country, was heading toward a massive heart attack. Clearly the time had come for whites to come out of denial and face up to the repercussions of the deep wounding we had caused, sometimes without consciousness, sometimes while willfully blind, and often purposefully.

Not all of the newspaper clippings and magazine articles that covered my desk had to do with violence. A significant number of writers focused on change—how to address racial issues in positive, proactive ways. In the *Huffington Post*, "Race and Repentance in America" appeared in October 2014. The author, Marianne Williamson, is best known for her spiritual teaching, her ten books, and her work to end poverty, create peace, and empower women. A few years later, she will run for president but in 2014 her article traces the history of slavery right up through institutionalized white supremacy and the high percentage of black children living in poverty. In so doing, she exposes the wounds undermining our society's best efforts at creating justice for all. She points out that an apology to blacks has never been made. "America needs to pay long overdue war reparations, and until we do, we will not move forward in any meaningful way. America needs more than forgiveness; we need genuine repentance, and restitution for our national sins."

That January, I checked into my hotel and stretched my legs on the sun-washed shoreline. Then I returned to my room. As synchronicity would have it, I turned on the Charleston ABC evening news channel just as Gregory came on and began reporting an unsolved murder case. He handled his interview well, confident and at ease—much more than I expected of one so fresh to the news business and so young.

The next day, Martin Luther King Jr. Day, Gregory drove out to Folly Beach to have dinner with me at my hotel. He came into the lobby with a wide grin, dressed in jeans with a dark blue button-down shirt, tie and vest. I walked right up and gave him a hug. It didn't seem as if almost two years had passed since I first met him in L.A.

We were ushered to a quiet table in Blu, the hotel restaurant. There was ample privacy embellished by the view of the sun taking its leave of the day in hues of peach and purple. Since Gregory doesn't drink, we went straight to the menu. He asked the waitress about specials and appeared to be well-versed in low country cuisine. Gregory smiled often, laughed with ease and seemed eager to talk with me. I asked him what his plans were for his next television job, noting that he was nearing the end of his two-year stint. I assumed he would go back to California. After explaining to me that there are 211 media markets in our country—New York is number one with the most media consumption; Los Angeles is number two, and Charleston is number 94— he told me that he would have to make at least two lateral moves before he could hope to go back to L.A. "My heart wants to go back to California. I love Cali, it's my home, my family is there and I'm very deeply rooted in my family." He also loves the pace and excitement of life in L.A. but wonders how he will get back to home ground. The magnetic pull of Miami and its Latin culture seemed to be on his mind as well. Whether he goes directly back to California or detours via Miami, he will move laterally from city to city until he reaches his goal.

I am naïve about his industry and assumed that he would be earning good money. But he said, "I make $27,000 a year so I don't take home a lot of money. If I renew, I'll still be making $30,000 or less even though I have two degrees and speak two languages." Scholarships and grants greatly reduced the cost of his education, but there still remains some student debt. Though he was frustrated and embarrassed by his earning level, he was proud to tell me that he is an MMJ, or multi-media journalist who shoots, edits, and writes his own stories.

In 2013, when I heard that Gregory would be going to Charleston for his first job, I gulped. "Out of the frying pan and into the fire" ran through my head. My own history with South Carolina started when I left Virginia after high school graduation and matriculated at Converse in Spartanburg, then a women's college for privileged white girls. In 1967 the prevailing trajectory for young women of my social class was to find a good man with earning potential, get married and have a family. If one felt compelled to work, nursing and teaching were the predominant viable options. Getting a college degree meant that status in our social group would be guaranteed. For many of us, it was an extension of high school, albeit a richer experience. My sophomore year, I jumped onto the newspaper staff, became editor and wrote anti-war pieces. Most of my classmates were unconcerned about the events taking place in Vietnam and probably didn't read a word I wrote. For me, South Carolina is one of those places where life doesn't change much. And I must admit that the vantage point from which I saw South Carolina then still shapes how I see the state today.

I had wondered how Gregory, brought up in the progressive culture of California, would fare in the still deeply southern and socially conservative atmosphere of Charleston. Now, almost two years later, I broached that issue with him. His response was sobering.

"I grew up in a neighborhood where… every house was a different culture, a different race, different something. I'm used to being in a multi-cultural, multi-dimensional environment. To come to Charleston, the Bible belt, where more than forty percent of the slaves came into America…. It's culture shock. It's depressing."

I looked into Gregory's eyes but could not discern just how profoundly he had been affected by his decision.

He referred to the history of Charleston as "a beautiful thing." Though he said this sincerely, I didn't see how he meant it. He bemoaned the fact that many of the people who live there haven't progressed in their thinking. "The history is their prime real estate in regard to tourism—people coming here. People's mentality is just so connected to the South that they can't imagine moving forward because they think that moving forward is letting go of the past."

To illustrate his point, he told me that he'd expected to see American flags flying about the city on July fourth, but instead Confederate flags were waving in full view. When he passed through Columbia, South Carolina, on his way to Charleston, he'd seen it ripple in the wind above the statehouse. The scene caused him to think, "Wow. I'm not welcomed here and it's going to be a long two years in this state."

I realized just how difficult life in Charleston had been for a sensitive yet determined twenty-five year old black man when he told me about the day he was reporting on Senator Lindsey Graham's campaign to block the White House-driven Affordable Care Act. Following Graham and his cohorts into the town hall, Gregory heard someone close by say, "We were just fine before Barack Obama got into office…. all the faggots, blackies and morons voted for him." Suddenly aware of Gregory's presence, the man turned to him and said, "But you don't want to hear what I have to say, boy." Gregory repeated these words just as he had heard them, hot and angry. My shame at the remark and the hurt I felt for Gregory caused me to react in judgment. Without saying it openly, I reverted to my own internalized discrimination and labeled the speaker as "poor white trash." Growing up in Mississippi, I was aware that the only label more offensive than "negro" was the one given to impoverished déclassé whites. The horror of Gregory's experience sickened me, but that did not justify my reversion to an old, pejorative stereotype that ironically refers right back to racism.

For the year and a half that Gregory had been working in Charleston, he'd swallowed comments that made him bristle and seethe. "Sometimes I feel less than a human being." As he explained it to me, he is a "quasi" public figure, so he can't express himself on or off the job. "(I) feel like, okay, keep your mouth shut, maintain composure and hold all of that in." Suddenly, I understood why I had not been able to connect with him over the preceding nine months. The previous spring I had invited Greg to Asheville and made other gestures to get together with him. He dodged me, and why wouldn't he have? Depressed and admittedly even suicidal, he reached out to the people he could trust the most, his pastor and his dad. Living alone, his thoughts threatened to get the best of him. He called his L.A. home, often in tears, saying "I can't stay here. I want to punch somebody in the face." But he hadn't. Instead he got into counseling and prayed harder. Now, with only six contractual months remaining, he could say to me, "I think I've gotten over it." I am sorry to say that words failed me at that moment. Instead of offering encouragement and support, I changed the subject. For fear of drowning, I could put only a toe into the river of his pain.

The brutal legacy of Charleston, "capital of the slave trade," lays its hands on the shoulders of blacks, young and old, to this day, and it still has the power to manipulate the thoughts, attitudes and sensibilities of southern whites. Those 400,000 Africans who stepped onto the auction block at the slave mart, many of whom stayed in South Carolina on plantations, were reminded every moment of every day that they were considered less than human and would be held in bondage and abused in countless ways. There had been 246 years of slavery before the Emancipation Proclamation and the end of the Civil War. During those years and afterward, blacks were put to work building the beautifully preserved pastel houses in downtown neighborhoods, with their lovely architectural features of Georgian, Federal and Greek Revival styles. Brick and stucco exteriors were built by slaves prior to the end of "the trade" in 1856. Black men, women and children worked the fields of rice plantations, and also served as blacksmiths, brick makers and domestics.

Charleston has developed a reputation as a major cultural center of the South, drawing international crowds to its seventeen day Spoleto Festival each spring, when world-renowned artists perform in venues throughout the city. Tourists revel in the lush gardens, the Civil War history, harbor sights along the battery, shopping in the Straw Market where sweet grass baskets harking back to African origins are for sale. Maybe Gregory's comment about the beauty of Charleston's history wasn't disingenuous at all. His home state of California wasn't acquired until 1848, some fifty-eight years after the Straw Market was established.

Our waitress came to the table with plates of steaming food. His lightly browned crab cakes atop a bed of salad greens arrived for Gregory, my order of sea scallops came next. It was a good time to back away from our conversation, to replenish body and soul. He'd offered to say grace, and I listened to his words while noting what seemed to me to be an anomaly. This hip, fit, together young black man, head bent in prayer, speaking freely and comfortably in a public setting, had suffered greatly, and I could hear it in his voice. It was clear to me that powerful forces within and without had shaped his life. I was grateful that he was so generous with his time and so forthcoming about his experience. We filled the space between us with less important topics. I had seen Facebook photos of Gregory with a couple of beautiful black women. When I mentioned them, he told me that he'd learned a lot about relationships. He said, "(My girlfriend) can't tell me in September that I did something wrong in March."

I wasn't sure what he meant by that.

He clarified. "I have to tell her, 'don't bottle it up and tell me months later what's bothering you.' I'm not that way. I may hold it in for a couple of days but it's not gonna be for months."

I responded that his approach seemed very healthy to me. My failed marriage was a testament to the dangerous practice of keeping a private grocery list of grievances.

He continued, "Yeah. I need a moment. I need a walk. I ask, 'Can we talk about it tomorrow.' Look at the career I'm in. It's a talking career."

When I asked him about the positive influence of his family, I heard his response with no small measure of surprise. "It wasn't a loving family that got me this far. I didn't feel loved in my family until I was grown."

"Tell me about it."

"It was wanting to escape that got me successful."

What? From the moment I met Gregory, his mother Latoya and his grandmother Pat, my impression was of a happy, supportive and loving family. Apparently that was not always the case. Three visits to L.A. had not revealed any reason to suspect otherwise except for one obvious chink: Virginia. While her crippled body confined her to bed and a solitary life, her children and grandchildren were afoot in the world, making their way as best they could.

When Gregory was a tyke, Latoya separated from his dad and fell in love. That relationship became her first marriage. As is so often the case, the dynamics of her home changed dramatically. Gregory spoke highly of his step-father and the liaison that lasted for twenty years. However, the step-siblings that came into his world made life almost unbearable for a time.

"I was the only one in the house that liked books and theatre. I didn't like sports. I didn't want to go out and run the streets. I was called a faggot, I was called gay and I was called a girl. I was overweight, had buck teeth and wore braces." Ouch. Even though he stressed the importance of Pat and his biological father—who "always had my back"— they were not living in close proximity so could not see the day-to-day results of his being bullied.

Now a bit older and wiser, he can understand why Latoya was sometimes unavailable to him. She worked full time, and she gave priority to her husband. "...There were just times when I felt like she loved my stepfather more than us or she took his side." I have heard this kind of thinking before from the children of mothers who remarry. It would be ill-advised for me to make an assumption that Gregory's perception was accurate but the feeling in him was genuine. Somehow he stayed focused on his schoolwork. He made exceptional grades and became involved in theatre and debate. Meanwhile he ascended to the position of number one debate champ in the state of California when he was in middle school. His family only attended one play and two debates. "I was the odd-ball step-child."

The meanness of Gregory's siblings did little to advance them in their lives. Their treatment of Gregory could easily have derailed him. One step-brother has been in jail for years. The older step-sister lives in the projects, and the younger step-brother was recently locked up. Gregory must have tried to fit in at one point, because his role evolved into that of chauffeur. When he drove his brothers to football practice and was sometimes out on the street with them, he saw frightening things. His sharpest memory arrived with sound effects. He heard the gun shot that propelled a bullet within inches of his right temple and ear. Gregory said, "With so much working against them —gang violence, drugs, lack of supervision, hunger, etc.— they end up doing dumb stuff and go to jail which is a modern day plantation where we are funneling kids to get them off the street."

Somehow Gregory had proven himself academically and avoided getting into trouble. While I listened to his story, I wondered how he had managed. After all, talents like those he possessed as a young boy don't thrive and grow in a vacuum. Latoya discouraged bad grades and wanted a better lifestyle for Gregory, but he was removed from his real supports, Pat and his father. There was likely someone, an independent source of encouragement also watching out for Gregory. It's usually someone in the educational system. And there was such a person in his life: Keynasia Buffong and her husband, Jonathan. When Gregory attended Rialto High School, he got to know the black school counselor. She took him under her wing and into her heart. She told him, "You have a lot going for yourself." She spoke to all of his teachers and visited his house. She made Gregory check in with her every week and he began to go to church with her. Because of her guidance and the mentorship of her husband, Gregory met kids who had a different value system. He said they were playful and full of pranks—they knew how to have good solid fun. Jonathan's spoken word team traveled throughout the state under the moniker "Project Action." The group conducted poetry and writing workshops. Gregory found a venue to express the trials and frustrations of his life. It was a healing experience for him. When he graduated from Clark University in Atlanta,

Keynasia was there. When he graduated from Berkeley, she was there. She flew him home from Atlanta to be in her wedding and when she discovered that Gregory was suffering from depression in Charleston, she offered to fly him back to L.A. again.

As he related this part of his story, Gregory softened, relaxed and smiled. He said, "I owe my life to them. I'd take a bullet for them. They are my saviors, guardian angels, godparents and the reasons I turned out different from my brothers."

Chapter 10

INCLUSION

While Gregory and I had our meal together on Folly Beach, one question continued to surface in my mind and threatened to hijack my attention. What is it going to take to create a culture that is safe and resistant to judgments based on skin color? Now that Gregory had been living in the South where he had experienced an old and tired regime, he might have an outsider's perspective to share.

First I wanted to know more about his Christian faith. From what I was able to discern, it seemed to be immensely important to him. I took the time to recall a story that his grandmother, Pat, had shared with me. She said that when Gregory was two years old, he ingested some rat poison. He was rushed to the hospital. Latoya was so distressed she couldn't stay in the room with her baby boy so she called her mother in distress. Pat hastened to the hospital, and she recalls the scene in his room. The doctor gave Gregory a healthy dose of tar, which when swallowed absorbed the poison. What stood out for her was his intense fear. He looked directly into her eyes, and she read there an uncanny reaction for one so small. She perceived that he didn't want her to show any emotion. He needed her strength to make everything all right so that he could be too. To Pat's way of thinking, this was a spiritual moment for Gregory. Latoya made sure that he went to church on Sundays, but Pat believes that his faith has its basis in personal choice.

She said that her number one grandson, her first, has always been sensitive to other people's eyes. "He is very observant."

She continued, "When he is frustrated, he calls me—no matter what the time of day, and he knows he can depend on me. I try to get him to be logical and to decrease his stress by talking things out. He'll be able to see things better and more clearly when he's not angry. Then he can make up his own mind and make better decisions. I don't guide him or tell him what to do." Pat's wisdom informs her own decisions and is well worth emulating. She tells Gregory that she's been through good times and bad, and she's thankful for all of it.

When I recounted this story to Gregory, he came out with a hearty laugh. "She never lets me forget the rat poison story."

After we finished eating, we watched the beach outside the window empty of people and dogs as nightfall approached. I mentioned to Gregory that I had been reading about reparations and asked how he thought our country might move toward healing.

When he answered me, I sensed that his whole body had tensed. "It's not going to change today. We are so separated by this race thing. I don't think we'll ever see it realized. It's just that simple." My first reaction was utter disappointment. Here is a black man just twenty-six years old, who does not have hope. I probed deeper, even though I had a nagging feeling that no black person, regardless of age, would tell me, a privileged white person, that change is going to come just because I so badly want to stop the machine that was started by my forefathers and that I have so haplessly ignored for the better part of my life. Ignored, yes. Somewhere in the collective unconscious of whites is a free floating sense of guilt. It's visceral, it's insidious, it's deadening to the soul. I know that my privileges growing up were not limited to my ability to go to good schools and have more than the basic necessities provided for me. My privilege allowed me to make judgments of fellow human beings based on their dark brown skin. I made assertions about their worth, their intelligence, their integrity without having to get to know them personally. This judgment thing that I have done and now strive mightily to avoid diminished me more than my black friend.

Gregory, it turns out, is a patient young man. He didn't want to talk about what we could do to make it better, but he was willing to try to help me understand. He said, "There is no central belief in the African American culture that there is a way for us to pull together and fight for what we want. We have one group of people who are sure that we have to take care of our own. We have another group of people that want to pretend that it (racism) doesn't exist, and they want to mix in with white culture –they don't want any part of a movement. There is no consensus among the black community. There is no real power."

I hadn't given much thought to the paralyzing effect of a race divided against itself. I think of it more in terms of anyone's right to their opinion, and to the fact that of course black people are not a homogenous whole. When I was teaching in a small private Episcopal elementary school, there had been one black student in my fifth grade class. He was the single black child in the whole school. Cornelius Moore, or "Corny" as the kids referred to him, was the only child born to a black couple who presented as most middle class whites do. They had good jobs, drove nice cars, and though I never went to their house, seemed to comfortably reside in our community, which at the time had a small black population living in substandard government housing. The Moores came to parent-teacher conferences like all the other parents but made very little noise. They were exceedingly proud of their son, who was a straight A student. Somehow, back in the 80s, it was possible for a small percentage of blacks to experience upward mobility. Remembering Cornelius led me to dig deeper into the disparity. I found a report issued by the Brookings Institute in 2013 that reported interesting figures. Back then and probably now, two out of three whites were able to ascend to the middle class by the time they reached middle age, while only three out of ten blacks could. It is important to bear in mind that Barack Obama was the first black person to reach the highest political position in the land. But what is happening to the 70% of African Americans who can't break out of poverty, who can't ascend in any way?

Gregory had much to say about this. "When you have gangs, drugs, low income housing—you have welfare programs, women having babies they can't take care of, you have a group of people who even if they wanted to stand up, don't have the ability to because they are in such a predicament that all they can think about is survival. And when you are in survival mode, you don't care about legislation, or fighting for something that can't be realized today, or seeing the effects of it til tomorrow." He suggested that black communities must coalesce to address the pernicious influence of guns, violence and drugs on black lives. He also believes that young black boys and girls need to be shown other routes. They need to be given opportunities to make a living wage so that life on the street will be less preferable than working within a mainstream system. When blacks can pay their rent, put food on their table, take care of their children without holding down three, four or five jobs, they will have energy to address some of these problems.

He looked directly at me and asked, "How do you expect a kid to do well in school when their mom is on crack, their dad is in jail and they don't know where the next meal is coming from? All they care about is lunchtime 'cause they can eat the only meal they might get all day." No wonder he has so little hope, I thought. But it wasn't until he opened up about his own experience that I began to appreciate just how remarkable Gregory really is. He told me that he had been shot at. He'd been jumped. In one incident, a gangster mistook him for a member of a rival gang. He would have been killed if a girlfriend hadn't jumped from the back seat of the car yelling, "No, not him." How was it even possible that he was sitting there with me?

Perhaps Gregory's mother explained the desperation best in her Facebook entry of April 28, 2015:

Unless you grew up in the 'hood' 'inner city' 'Urban' areas 'under- served community' or whatever else it's called; it will be impossible to understand the aggression, and pent up anger when its triggered. I grew up in the Daryl Gates LAPD gang era. It was open season on every black/Latino male in the hood. Black males were constantly robbed and beat up by the LAPD (I'm sure I can throw in a few murders). Innocent men are still in prison today as a result of the corruption in the late 80's-90's. Take LAPD corruption and multiply that by every hood in America… Voila…. You have people who unleash rage in the most destructive form. People don't just wake up hoping to burn a neighborhood. But I'm certain that as long as these suspicious deaths continue to happen to black men at the hands of the law…the rage will continue to unleash with no control.

As I reflected on Latoya's post, I wondered how the parents of victims of police brutality had managed to maintain their dignity. In the immediate aftermath of the killings, when they were numb and in shock, they often called for peaceful protest. They had the strength to tamp down their anger and the hope that justice would be served. But would they be able to continue in the face of a barrage of incidents?

September 4, 2014

Levar Jones survived after being shot multiple times by a South Carolina state trooper.

December 2

Rumain Bisbon dies after fleeing arrest. No charges were brought against a white Phoenix police officer.

March 1, 2015

Charly "Africa" Keunang, a homeless man in Los Angeles was shot and killed by police officers.

March 6

Naeschylus Vinzant, an unarmed black man in Aurora, Colorado, was killed by policemen.

March 6

Tony Robinson of Madison, Wisconsin, was shot by Officer Matt Kenny.

March 9

Anthony Hill, a black Air Force veteran living in Chamblee, Georgia, dies when shot by white police officer.

Later, as I reflected on Gregory's inability to believe that a brighter future was possible during his lifetime, I became increasingly uncomfortable about the life I had known. It was hard to dodge a more overt sense of guilt for my privilege. I had a responsibility to take a hard look at it and make some changes.

A good friend told me about the 16th annual White Privilege Conference that was scheduled to take place in Louisville, Kentucky, March 11-14, 2015. A cursory glance at the WPC website revealed an amazing offering of workshops, fifteen to twenty each day. The choices were overwhelming. I was fearful. What if I got there and walked into a mass of angry people who saw me as the perfect "poster child" for the privileged white class. The logical part of my brain stepped in. *Whoa. This is not just about you.*

Typically, when I resist a "golden" opportunity out of fear, God nudges me forward. This time the nudge came in the form of a black woman, a poet from Boulder, Colorado, Norma Johnson. The same friend who told me about the WPC, also introduced me to Norma. I sent her a copy of *Death in the Delta* and she sent me to a Youtube video performance of her—"Poem for My White Friends: I Didn't Tell You."

From the start, we had rapport and respect for each other. After reading my book, Norma said, "I hope you are experiencing some joy in this journey." She prepared me for what was to come at the WPC. In an email she wrote, "There are amazing folks of all backgrounds. It's a juicy time. You won't have any trouble connecting with committed, creative people that share your intention. You'll feel yourself welcomed 'home' to a community that shares the heart of the adventure you're on."

I walked into the conference site on Thursday, March 12th, with 1700 other people. Some came from colleges and universities, some were members of coalitions working for equity and social justice... everyone seemed to be committed to building relationship, accountability and responsibility. Though I have no data to back up my calculations, it seemed to me that about 60% of attendees were black. The rest were white, Native American, or immigrant. Like a beehive in the spring, the conference center was a busy place. People were working hard to collaborate so as to bridge the divides along color lines, religious lines, gender lines, any place where those lines intersected.

The keynote speaker, Loretta Ross, addressed an impassioned audience. She has an impressive list of accomplishments and is not only a model of resilience, having survived numerous traumatic events as a young woman, but she also has the ability to marshal the language necessary to elucidate the old, tired and loaded problems of racial history in our country. Her forte is her ability to facilitate communication and open up dialogue between beleaguered individuals. I came away with a better understanding of white privilege and white supremacy. She said, "Everybody swims in a sea of white supremacy. How do we start to clean up the pollution in that water? We start with shared definitions and a commitment to 'Call people in. Don't call people out.'" For me, this lecture crystallized the purpose of my going to WPC: to become more conscious and aware of the needs and the rights of those people who struggle. It was not comfortable to have my eyes opened. There is no easy fix for the multi-layered system that is racism. And yet, sitting in the throngs of people that day felt safe and more importantly, honest.

If Loretta's speech was enlightening for me, the first session I attended after it, held out more hope than I could have imagined. How I decided to hear Dr. William "Smitty" Smith, I don't really know except for three words that jumped out in the title of the workshop: A Look at the Resistance, Action, Courage, & Equity of **White Southern Allies**—Past and Present..." When he said, "There's always been a moral counterweight to racism… a close cross cultural, cross racial collaboration and friendship," my vision blurred with tears. For nine years, I had been coming to terms with the devastating discovery that my family had been swept up in the deep southern racist framework. Yet, I also witnessed a shared and protective, nurturing and even respectful attitude that lived in my family alongside egregious and hostile acts. Here was a learned black man talking about individual whites who aided and abetted black women and men in their struggle for freedom.

After listening to stories of grass roots efforts such as the cross-racial collaboration taking place in my birth state, Mississippi, I began to see some strains of light coming up on the horizon. Though my relationship with Pat, Latoya, Gregory, and Virginia bent toward friendship from the beginning, amity with blacks where I live, in North Carolina, has seemed a distant prospect, not because I am not open to it; but because I have felt that I would not be accepted. Dr. Smith remarked that for there to be public discourse and collaboration we need to move beyond the blame/grievance cycle. I would add that we need to move beyond guilt, and that can't happen until there is reconciliation.

So much of what I was learning had to do with communication and the following workshop, about conversation, was led by a teacher and outreach specialist from the Seattle Girls' School. She had very good advice about how to speak from the heart, how to listen and other valuable skills that we have and use but need to be reminded of from time to time.

Over the course of the following days, my understanding of white privilege deepened and I learned more terminology that I could apply to dialogue. Perhaps the most uncomfortable self-discovery that I made was that if I remain silent in situations where active prejudice is present, if I don't speak out, it is as if I am hiding behind my privilege, and that protects it. If I continue to live an insular life, racially comfortable and removed from stress, my white fragility will only exacerbate defensiveness and the consensus that it is better to be white.

April 4

Charleston, South Carolina. Officer Michael Slager
is caught on video in the shooting death of Walter
Scott. Scott died after eight bullets to the back.

Gregory was first to report on ABC news that Walter Scott
had died. I was only home from the White Privilege Conference a matter of weeks when the news broke. Just when
I thought I was part of a groundswell that promised something positive and good, my hopes were crushed. Another
black man down.

Chapter 11

CHARLESTON

———— ∞∞∞ ————

AFTER I RETURNED TO ASHEVILLE, I READ THROUGH the notes I took while talking with Gregory. Something he had said made me think of his California family. Gregory would not have known Virginia's husband, Charlie Lee Jr., because he died in the 80s before Gregory was born. But Charlie Lee Sr., known to the children as Big Pops, lived on 130th Street in Compton until he died. Gregory remembered him sitting in his favorite chair with a big bottle of jellybeans nearby. Big Pops picked out the purple ones because he knew Gregory didn't like them. Memories like that one seemed to be sustaining him in the absence of day to day family contact.

The last thing Gregory said to me after we had dinner together at Folly Beach was a play on a cliché: What happens in black families, stays in black families. In this way, blacks and whites are similar except that historically, at least in our country, the need to keep family matters out of the public arena was imperative for the safety of blacks. Take the community response to Simon's death. White people didn't talk about it, but instead pretended it didn't happen. Blacks sequestered themselves in their homes and circulated the story privately. Any open discussion would have aroused suspicion or retaliation.

Gregory had hinted about a piece of his family's story that was a tender spot—mostly for Pat.

In the late 80s when Pat was about thirty-five, she was working two jobs. Her father was dead, and Virginia was living in an apartment alone. Since Pat had started having children when she was sixteen, by this time, she was finished with childrearing, her second marriage was over and she was working. "I was doing nicely," she told me.

Then she met Dennis after she moved into an apartment next door to him. At first, they became friends. Pat warmed to him because he offered to help out. When she wrecked her car, he said, "I can get you to a good mechanic." Later, while she was working in her yard and garden, he offered to help her with the planting.

"You'll get dirty," she said.

He responded, "I don't mind getting dirty." Pat sized him up to be "nice" and "genuine." They dated for the following two years.

In the meantime, Pat was caring for Virginia. She watched as her mother's body deteriorated and became less functional. Pat also took pains to keep up with Charlie Lee Sr. One day when Pat visited him, he said, "Stay here and save your money. You pay $1400 for rent and you're living like a movie star out in Hollywood." Dennis didn't appreciate Charlie Lee's intrusion into Pat's private affairs, but ultimately she told her grandfather she would move to Compton. Not one full day before her actual move, Charlie Lee died unexpectedly of a massive stroke. That morning when he awoke his breathing had become labored. He said, "I'm okay, it's a cold." But as he waited for his neighbor to arrive and take him to the doctor, he felt increasing irritation for the delay. Perhaps hypertension was partially at fault when he collapsed.

After Pat settled into the new rancher, she married Dennis. It was bad enough that he had pulled a "bait and switch" on her—his "nice words" turned caustic– but soon enough he was also selling drugs in the neighborhood. Strange people started coming to the house, so Pat's sense of safety and her value system were compromised. Her belief that she and Dennis would be happy began to erode as well.

During those early years of her marriage, Pat continued to push her body through strenuous exercise even though she had had the serious back injury while working at Lucky's. When Pat felt the pain "come out of nowhere," that's when I changed my diet and exercise routine to keep my back strong." Careful not to overdo, Pat improved but she knew there were grave consequences to losing her health. She told me, "I realized I didn't want to get sick under Dennis' watch because he would have women in the house." That's when she filed for divorce. Dennis was resistant and claimed he had ownership in the house because he had contributed a small amount of money to it. He demanded that she give him $100,000. Pat's attorney assured her that she only had to pay interest on his investment, but that wasn't enough to make Dennis move from the property. In that sense, the workman's compensation that Pat acquired after her injury was both a blessing and curse. Dennis knew he could threaten Pat and she would eventually cave in. She offered him $25,000 but in the end had to divide the claims payment with him. It sounded like extortion to me. When Pat told me this part of her story, just a couple of years after she had gained her freedom and independence, she shared a conversation she'd had with the Lord. "You knew what I needed before I knew what I needed. I needed a good spanking and you gave it to me. I get it. I get it. You don't have to tell me no more."

I love being a Journalist .. It's the first draft of history .. But covering the #BlackLivesMatter movement sometimes got me thinking less about work & more about how proud I am this movement is really gaining grounds .. I just keep singing "It's been a long time coming, but I know, a change gone come!"

North Charleston, South Carolina. On April 4, 2015, a fifty-year-old black man named Walter Scott was driving with a broken brake light when he was pulled over for questioning by a white police officer, Michael Slagel, age thirty-three. At the time, Walter was employed as a forklift operator. He was the father of four children and was engaged to be married. This was not his first encounter with the law. Indeed, he had been arrested ten times for minor offenses and appeared in court multiple times due to failure to pay child support. His cousin later told the press, "Walter was a nice, good, honest person…He was a grown man working hard to take care of his family." Both Walter and Michael had served in the Coast Guard until honorably discharged.

Michael Slager took the oath of office and joined the Charleston police squad on March 1, 2010. He had a good reputation for safety tactics, but had two formal complaints filed against him, one for the use of excessive force. At home, his wife was expecting a child in one month. On this fateful day he stopped Walter Scott for questioning. The dashboard camera in his cruiser recorded a routine encounter but for some unknown reason, Walter's fear got triggered. Speculation has it that what motivated Walter to suddenly turn and run from the squad car was fear that nonpayment of child support would lead to his arrest. Another source revealed that Slager reached for his Taser before resorting to deadly force, as is mandated by police policy. Walter may have had a deeper concern more endemic in black culture. Attorney Benjamin Crump, who represented the families of Trayvon Martin, Michael Brown and Tamir Rice, wrote in the April 20, 2015 issue of *Time,* "There is a blanket of distrust, disrespect and indifference that has been thrown across black men in America. And it is resulting in too many deaths at the hands of armed police officers who claim they are afraid."

When Walter fled across a nearby open field, Michael Slager jumped from his cruiser, drew his weapon, and fired eight bullets. Four of them entered Walter's back and one hit his ear. While he lay face down on the ground, he was handcuffed. Slager made little effort to provide Walter with medical attention. Then, he ran back to his cruiser, retrieved his Taser and quickly dropped it close to Walter's body. Already he had framed a story that was untrue. He made a call into headquarters and said, "I had to use my weapon." In his *Time Magazine* article, Benjamin Crump wrote, "Far too often the police come up with the same narrative: I felt threatened, I felt afraid, the victim struggled with me, he reached for my gun. This is the same old story from officers who shoot unarmed black men." Slagle stated in his police report that there had been a shuffle; that Walter had gotten control of his Taser; that he fired in self-defense.

At just about the same time as the incident involving Walter Scott, Gregory was in his car driving to the scene of a homicide in Mount Pleasant, a large suburb to the north of Charleston's city center, but his assignment was derailed when a text arrived from his producer, Jasmine Hooks. Gregory called her and she responded, "There's been a shooting in North Charleston. On the scanner I heard the officer say he had to use his gun. Get there now! This could be big."

Gregory's automatic response was to "bust it" to the scene, and he got there three hours ahead of any other news personnel. Stretched out in an ambulance was the body of Walter Scott. Medics were making a valiant effort to revive him but it wasn't working. Yellow caution tape was "everywhere." Gregory went right to work, interviewing witnesses and police. He also began to tweet and post on Facebook, using social media to get the story out there before any other reporters could. Before he left the scene, he saw the ambulance carry Walter away. What he did not know at that time would become critical to the future of police work in this country. One witness of the crime did not come forward with the others that Gregory spoke to; he had been riding his bike near the crime scene, and he filmed the death of Walter Scott on his cell phone.

THE YEAR 2015 WAS SHAPING UP TO BE CATACLYSMIC in terms of violent racially charged incidents. In April, after Walter Scott died, I contacted Gregory and made plans to meet him in Folly Beach again the next month. We planned to meet at the popular restaurant "The Lost Dog" at lunchtime. This encounter with Gregory was both timely and providential. Within a matter of weeks Charleston would be under siege, and Gregory would be swept up in an historic moment.

When we met that May day, Gregory became increasingly excited as he recounted the drama that followed the shooting. He spoke fast. His voice grew louder. He leaned close to the table, his back rigid. I listened intently because the noise level in the restaurant was making it hard to hear each other. At times, I had to lean in over my lunch plate.

Gregory had experienced success working with teenagers when he lived in Los Angeles and that became an important asset. In the little bit of spare time that he had in Charleston, he volunteered at Stall High School. For the Wisest Warriors program at Stall, he helped students who were behind in their reading. His presence around the school caught the attention of one of the vice-principals and they became friends. The night of Walter Scott's shooting, Gregory got a text message: "Hey. There's a Dominican guy who has a video. He recorded it all and what the cell video shows doesn't line up with the police report. So I'm trying to find out if he would be willing to talk." They set up a meeting for later the next day, a Sunday. Gregory's producer called on him to report on all sorts of gatherings for Walter Scott, whose family would be going to church and on to a vigil.

Meanwhile Gregory was in touch with Muhiyidin D'Baha, the local leader of the Black Lives Matter group. D'Baha knew about the video too and was concerned that it might get into the wrong hands, for example, those of the police. Gregory showed up at the vigil, keenly aware of the explosive evidence the family was keeping sequestered. He noticed Walter's brother abruptly leave the vigil, so he followed him and watched the brother get in a car with the same people who told him about the video. With stealth, Gregory followed them at a safe distance, managing to get to the gathering place undetected by anyone outside the inner circle. When he arrived, he found himself in the company of Walter's brother, the vice principal of Stalls High School, O'Baha, and Feidin Santana (the 23 year old videographer who was a barber, well known in the Latino community). As the only media rep, Gregory was the obvious person to take possession of the evidence, but the family had something else in mind: they wanted to give it to their attorney so that no one, including Feidin, would become vulnerable to danger at the hands of the police.

On the spot, Gregory got his boss at the news station on the phone. "Hey, there's a video and they're saying this video will show the truth of what happened but they are not giving it away for free. Are you willing to pay for it?" He handed his phone to the vice principal so that negotiations could continue.

To Gregory's disappointment, his producer told him that the news director wouldn't pay for the video because it was unethical. Soon after, calls went out to Channel 2 and Channel 5, but they too were unwilling to pay for the evidence. In the end, the video wound up at ABC in New York and with the *New York Times*. Then it went viral and everyone in the country was able to see the raw coverage of the incident. On CNN, Monday, April 13, Feidin appeared in an interview with Anderson Cooper, who when reviewing the footage, pointed out that Feidin moved closer to the scene as it unfolded. "Were you scared?" he asked. Feidin, dressed neatly in a tan button–down shirt, composed and respectful, answered, "No." He said he never expected to see something like that happen right in front of him. Acting on impulse, he ignored the threat of danger, moved in closer and recorded the scene.

Gregory didn't hold back his frustration when telling me about the media side of Walter Scott's murder. About Feidin, he said, "I found him. No one knew he existed. I knew about it first....but the big guys had it. So here's Lester Holt (ABC News) walking around with Feidin but I already had the name and the video, but we just couldn't pay for it. They gave it to me first." Prior to national attention, Feidin was afraid for his life. He was hiding out at his friend's house in Summerville, outside the city limits of Charleston and in a place where people wouldn't seek to find him. That friend happened to be a production assistant at Greg's news station—Raphael, from Puerto Rico. At work, he didn't say anything about the video because he didn't want to lose Feidin's trust. Greg said, "All of the connections were at our news station."

Gregory finally took a break from telling me the story. I straightened up and waited until I had his full attention. "Gregory, have you had time to process what happened to Walter Scott?"

"No. We are just so short-staffed at the station. I was up and at the office at 3:00. They had me on the air at 5, 5:30, 6, 6:30, 7, 10:00 and 11:00 and then the news for 6 and 7 o'clock all week. It was big. It was big."

"Yes, it was, but I'm remembering something else that was big. Think about it. Your great-great grandfather just home from the service in World War II was shot in the back as he fled a honky tonk in Anguilla, Mississippi. My father and his brothers arrived on that scene as a self-appointed posse. They were armed. Simon was not. He was gunned down and left to die face down in the dusty street. Gregory responded with his whole body. His hands came down to the table. He sat all the way back in his chair—the air

Molly Walling

rushed out of his lungs. I was looking into the face of a sober, pensive young man who had absolutely no words for the next few minutes.

When he spoke again, it was to tell me about the consequences of the tragedy. The Reverend Jesse Jackson, born in Greenville, South Carolina, had donated $1000 to the Charleston chapter of Black Lives Matter as seed money for a project called "We Are Watching You." Those involved checked crime statistics to find out high crime areas in the city. Subsequently, trainers from Ferguson, Missouri, traveled to Charleston to train members of Black Lives Matter in police surveillance. In this program, individuals go into rough neighborhoods between 8:00 and 10:00 o'clock at night with cameras. According to Gregory, "When they see sirens, they film basic police stops and then look for discrepancies between police incident reports and what they recorded." North Charleston's Mayor, Keith Summey and the Chief of police stated that they were going to hold a city council meeting specifically for police reform. He announced that body cameras had been ordered.

I asked if things had begun to settle down after so much national attention. It would be another three weeks before Slagel was indicted for the murder of Walter Scott.

Gregory explained, "You see a community awaken slowly… a very docile community in regard to going about change in a politically correct way. Now everyone has had to go on back to their lives. There weren't the numbers of people out there as there should have been. They care just as much, but they don't have it in them to mobilize. They are just not fed up enough to go Hughey Newton crazy and say, 'This has got to stop.'"

No one suspected that systems would begin in fail on such a massive scale as they did in the beautiful old city of Charleston in the spring and early summer of 2015. The shooting death of Walter Scott was the first major crack along a centuries old fault line. What came next brought the nation to its knees.

WHILE GREGORY WAS DOING MARATHON REPORTING on the Walter Scott case, his mother Latoya was back home in L.A. crafting her own creative response to the horrors unfolding in early 2015. On Facebook she posted this:

> Gyrl Talk Awareness Brunch
> Enjoy a fun, Mother-Daughter event designed to open communication and increase awareness of tough issues our girls are faced with today. Guest Speakers will share expert knowledge in the topics of Domestic Violence and Teens and Sex Trafficking. Material is appropriate for attendees ages 12 and up....

On June 13, Latoya's event took place with a sold out crowd of girls. Her three hour program included small group dis-cussions covering sensitive issues that are typically loaded with pressure from peers and others. She brought in experts who could give the girls valuable tools to be used in deci-sion-making; she provided lunch, games and raffles. In her own words, "Because the workshops are small, I have the opportunity to reach everyone in the room. No one will be lost in the crowd." It seemed paramount to Latoya that the participants would go home with a heightened sense of confidence and greater self-worth. "My hope is, through

Molly Walling

Gyrl Talk, the Wise Women will take a more assertive stance in sharing their wisdom and teach our young girls how to grow into confident women." I studied the photographs Latoya posted on line. In one, I found Pat standing in the group, witnessing the good work of her daughter.

Gregory's family in California was stepping up to be a force for good, just as he was doing in Charleston. It may take thousands of tiny "villages" working at the grass roots level to bring about change. Every effort builds on what has gone before. Gregory pointed out to me that the trajectory of change that launched in Ferguson, Missouri, was based on the "Black Lives Matter," movement that started after the Trayvon Martin case. Following that, the incident in New York with Eric Garner produced, "I can't breathe." Then, a video that captured the death of Walter Scott resulted in "Do you believe us now."

Only eight days after Walter Scott's death, Freddie Gray died in Baltimore, and six police officers were charged. This time the victim fled, was captured and roughed up while being transported in a police vehicle. He suffered from injuries to his neck and spine. His condition deteriorated into a coma and he died one week later in the hospital. After the funeral, protests erupted spontaneously, causing major destruction of property. In the following days, twenty police were injured and 250 arrests were made. On April 28, the riots ended. On April 29, over 200 businesses were unable to reopen. The very public response to Freddie's death happened almost instantaneously. Gregory postulated, "I don't think Baltimore would have happened the way it did if it weren't for Walter Scott." Clearly Feidin's video made a bruised and battered black population even more sensitive to the mistreatment they were experiencing at the hands of police. By the time this happened, I was moving through an avalanche of emotions, and other white people of conscience were surely doing the same. One minute I felt shocked, the next aggrieved, then scared—scared to turn on the television, to listen to NPR. I wanted to put my head under the nearest pillow and wait out this firestorm of racial tension. When I wrote *Death in the Delta*, I had to work through deep regret and shame that my family had participated in the subjugation, oppression and even killing of two black men. This year, 2015, was taking me back to a time when I was so vulnerable I could hardly stand to think about it.

Chapter 12

WHAT CAN HAPPEN
IN CHURCH

The church is and always has been the center of African-American life—a place to call our own in a too often hostile world, a sanctuary from so many hardships. ...They have been, and continue to be, community centers where we organize for jobs and justice; places of scholarship and network; places where children are loved and fed and kept out of harm's way, and told that they are beautiful and smart and taught that they matter. That's what happens in church.

PRESIDENT OBAMA, CHARLESTON,
JUNE 26, 2015

Molly—I keep hearing Charleston referred to as the Holy City. What's that about?

Gregory—We are in the heart of the Bible Belt. The skyline of Charleston cannot exceed the height of the tallest church building. It has to do with historic preservation.

FOR SIMON   153

YES, THE NAME DOES HAVE TO DO WITH THE SKYLINE but other theories are circulating in response to this question. Charleston's reputation begins with religious tolerance as evidenced by the rich and varied houses of worship built within a relatively small area. Also, steeples visible at sea helped ship captains guide their vessels into the Charleston harbor.

The morning of June 17th began for me as most others. I arose from bed, made myself presentable enough to take my dog, Toby, out for his morning constitutional before setting out a cup full of kibbles. After that I poured myself a bowl of cereal, turned on my coffee-maker and set the channel on the Bose to the local NPR station. Already the sun was bearing down with intense heat and a blanket of humidity pressed uncomfortably close. Earlier in the week two Supreme Court rulings surprised most Americans and prompted the radio pundits to spin out their views. One was the landmark decision to allow same-sex couples to marry. That certainly could be viewed as a thumbs up for equality. Then the Supreme Court Justices upheld the Affordable Care Act, the centerpiece of Obama's legislative efforts to provide health insurance for people who don't have workplace coverage.

Starting my day, knowing that positive change was afoot, I felt hopeful and relaxed. While I ate breakfast, I gazed out the window into my kitchen garden where impossibly tall red, pink and yellow "state pride" zinnias stretched sunward. Then the "Morning Edition" newscast was interrupted with late breaking news—from Charleston.

The previous evening, a prayer group had gathered at the 199 year old Emanuel AME Church in Charleston's historic district. The pastor, Clemente Pinckney, 41, was leading the all black group when a 21 year old white man entered the room and sat down with them. The young man with light brown hair in a bowl cut and sad, dead eyes sunken into dark circles, sat amid the gathering for almost an hour. Then, as dispassionately as if he were pouring a cup of coffee, Dylann Roof removed a .45 caliber handgun from his pocket, took aim, and pulled the trigger at close range on nine people in the room. He killed them, one at a time, firing into the bodies more than once to make sure they were dead. One person was injured but survived the attack. Before Roof fired, he uttered these words, "You rape our women and you're taking over our country." Clemente Pinckney, who was much beloved by blacks and whites in Charleston, was killed. Other victims included: Tywanza Sanders, 26; Cynthia Hurd, 54; Sharonda Coleman-Singleton, 45; Rev. Daniel Lee Simmons, Sr. 74; Susie Jackson, 87; DePayne Middleton-Doctor, 49; Ethel Lance, 70. Somehow I swallowed a mouthful of cereal before involuntarily crying out, "Oh no. No. No. No." My instinct was to break something, to slam my fist down on the tabletop, to run down the street yelling at no one. Instead, I reined in my shock, then listened to the broadcast to ascertain the details of what happened. In my head, the word "why" was on continuous loop. And, *What about Gregory? How will this affect him? Will he be in danger out there in public reporting on this?*

Throughout the course of researching and writing my family's story, one fact has become abundantly clear: black churches have always been safe havens where people could let down their guard and be themselves because they knew that in the eyes of God, there was no discrimination—only love. This young white man, full of hate, had violated a sacred space, destroying the sense of security in every single gathering place for people of color.

I was relieved on one hand that the perpetrator was working solo, but knowing that Dylann Roof chose to make his assault in a place where blacks were most vulnerable made me ill. Nine people were shot in a space made sacred by almost two hundred years of prayer, while entering into direct communication with their Creator. As the media released a clearer profile of Roof, I learned that he had originally planned to make an assault on The College of Charleston but was unsuccessful due to security. Investigators discovered that he had a fascination with white supremacy and neo Nazism. He had flags of racist Rhodesia and apartheid South Africa sewn to his jacket. His online manifesto indicated his choice of Charleston because it is the oldest city in South Carolina. His actions were motivated by intense hatred, allowed to ferment in the grip of mental illness.

In the following hours, I was too paralyzed to do anything except follow the news loop. President Obama said in a press conference, "I've had to make statements like this too many times." More than the words, his posture, sadness, and resolve indicated that he was deeply affected by the senseless deaths. David Remnick, editor of *The New Yorker*, wrote of Obama's speech,

> ...he insisted that mass killings, like the one in Charleston, are, in no small measure, political. This is the crucial point. These murders were not random or merely tragic; they were pointedly racist; they were political. Obama made it clear that the cynical actions of so many politicians—their refusal to cross the N.R.A. and enact strict gun laws, their unwillingness to combat racism in any way that puts votes at risk—have bloody consequences.

Later in the day, South Carolina Governor, Nikki Haley, made her statement while trying but failing to rein in her emotions. She said, "We all woke up today and the heart and soul of South Carolina was broken." Her sentiments were genuine, and she would in the coming days be moved to take unusual action for a Republican governor in the deep South—to remove the Confederate flag from the grounds of the state capitol.

The next day in the local news, I read that the St. James AME church near downtown Asheville would hold a service. I wanted to drive to Charleston, but I had been there so recently, and there would be no chance of seeing Gregory, so I stayed close to home. The service at St. James two days after the massacre gave me an opportunity to experience healing power at work in a black sanctuary. Every pew was full. People of all colors filled the nave and spilled out the doors and onto the street. On one side of the chancel, Randy Weston and other musicians sent blue notes out over the people. Instrumental spirituals created a quieting effect. Later they amped up the cadence and volume to rouse us to our feet. The program was titled "We Are Charleston: A Service of Solidarity and Healing."

For the Reverend LaPrince Edwards, this was especially true. He was raised in the Mother Emanuel Church and knew each of the nine people murdered there. When he first began to preach, his emotion was raw and threatened to end his sermon prematurely, but he didn't let it. First he cautioned the congregation that what happened in Charleston could have happened anywhere. He pressed in with the admonition that it is time for people to come together, to drop all divisions and "not just have talk and rhetoric but a real plan of action" because if we stop being afraid to admit the fact that racism is still alive and well in America, then there is hope.

In the crowd of strangers, I felt welcome. The music, the scripture readings, and the overt physical displays of faith and spirit that would have been uncomfortable for me at one time were nourishing at that moment. As the pitch of the sermon became more intense, people rose to their feet. When Rev. Edwards said, "We are resilient and full of hope—the best is yet to come," his words were a comfort to me and I suspect to everyone in the congregation that day.

The following afternoon a bond hearing was held for Dylann Roof, who had been captured near Shelby, North Carolina, after fleeing the bloody scene at Emanuel. Family members of the nine murder victims could see and speak with Roof by means of a video screen on the wall of the courthouse. Not only did they cry about the loved ones they had lost, but they offered Roof forgiveness. When I first heard this, I paused. Yes, it was a beautiful thing to think that the people most affected by the deaths could bring themselves to look the murderer in the eye and say words like, "I forgive you. You took something very precious away from me. I will never talk to her...ever again. I will never be able to hold her again. But I forgive you....God forgive you." Yes, it was a beautiful thing. But...when I tried to put myself in their place, I couldn't understand how they could say these words, much less genuinely mean them. Would their gesture have any effect on someone so full of hatred? Did that even matter? For me, it has taken years to come to forgive significant people who have harmed me. As I watched the scene unfold, I struggled with my apparent weakness of faith and character. I found some answers in the July 2 issue of the *Nation*.

In her article titled: "Why the Black Church Forgives Dylann Roof," Kelly Douglas Brown, Goucher College Professor of Religion, helped me to understand from the perspective of black theology. She wrote:

> While the meaning of forgiveness in black church faith is complex, such forgiveness is not about the exoneration of the killer for the deadly injustice he allegedly perpetrated. Rather, it is about the loving justice of God and the liberation of the families from the killer's sinful act.
>
> Forgiveness, in the first instance, recognizes that no human justice can adequately respond to the grave injustice of such a racist, terroristic, murderous crime. Forgiveness, then, is a sign of the families' faith that God's justice will ultimately prevail and thus, it frees them from the anguish of knowing that no human justice will make up for the loss of their family members.
>
> Secondly, forgiveness frees the families from being trapped in the cycle of the alleged killer's hate. Forgiveness is not a palliative for rightful anger and rage; instead it frees the families from the kind of hate that not only distorts their own sense of self but also prevents them from moving forward in their own living. But most importantly, forgiveness recognizes that the love of God is more powerful than white racist hatred. In the end, forgiveness within the black faith tradition liberates black people to continue to persevere in the struggle for freedom from the sinful realities of white racism.

Although Kelly Douglas Brown's exposition on forgiveness was one I could wrap my head around, it wasn't until further inquiry that I discovered a more grievous truth. Once again my life as a privileged white American had protected me from knowing a darker aspect of black faith. Throughout history, black Americans have been expected to absolve white Americans of their crimes. Without having had an inkling of my own culpability, I have participated in a culture that allows me an unearned and undeserved expectation that blacks will forgive me no matter what I say or do to them.

I looked at the stoic presence of affected family members in the Charleston Courthouse. Memory took me back nine years to Anguilla, Mississippi, where I met with Simon Toombs' nieces and with 93 year old King Evans, a witness to Simon's 1946 death. They had what seemed like an intense need for me to understand that after the sheriff took my father into custody, each and every black person in that community withdrew into their homes knowing that to speak out would jeopardize their safety and make them somehow complicit in a perceived backlash. From the day the first Africans stepped onto our shore, there hasn't been a moment when they were safe from physical and mental abuse, dispossession of all they had, oppression both social and institutional. And if that wasn't hard enough, they were expected to excuse the people who wronged them.

What if Sheriff Crawford had arranged for Simon's and David's families to come into the courthouse so that they could speak to my father and his brothers. How would Dad have reacted to them? To being told, "I forgive you for taking my son, brother, father, away from me forever." Somehow I can't seem to walk into that scene in my mind's eye. I can say with clarity that my dad was capable of reacting with shame and guilt. But today, as I contemplate the actions of the families in Charleston, I understand that it wasn't only a Biblical strong-arm that compelled them to forgive Roof, it was also forced on them by our culture.

On the day of Reverend Pinkney's funeral, I caught a glimpse of Gregory on Channel 4 news. The throngs who hoped to enter the College of Charleston TD Arena were huge; some people waited in line for hours. Once the arena was full, many who hadn't been able to get in gathered around the AME Church where Gregory interviewed them. "How do you feel about being turned away from the funeral?" he asked. One man answered with resolve that though he had stood outside in the scorching heat for hours, he would simply go home and watch the funeral on his TV. And that is what I did too.

Numerous eloquent tributes were paid to Clemente Pinckney before President Obama's concluding oratory. Dylann Roof and others of his supremacist stripe were feeling threatened by the shift of power away from whites as represented by Obama's election. But Roof's timing could not have served him worse. Six and a half years into a second term, Obama was in the home stretch. He had, up until this time, parsed his words with extreme care so as not to inflame racial tensions. On this day, June 19, 2015, Obama allowed himself to look directly into the cold eyes of racism. Without flinching, he named it; he spoke truthfully about the problems of race that need to be addressed; he talked about the birthright of extreme cruelty and murder that continue to wound our nation. Obama spoke of his own diverse ethnic background, and he followed up by singing "Amazing Grace" a cappella. Along with the congregation and millions of Americans watching from home, I could not take my eyes off the screen. I could not cry. Awe and admiration flooded through me and I knew that at the very least, the city of Charleston and all who love her had their hearts opened wider that day.

Proof of this came two days later when a peaceful protest occurred. The skyline of the city is accented by the arch of the Arthur Ravenel Bridge. Finished in 2005, the cable-stayed expanse connects downtown Charleston with Mount Pleasant. It is a sight to behold. Police accompanied a crowd that ranged between 10,000 to 15,000 people, who carried a banner stating, "Love Never Fails. Charleston Strong." The causeway was impassable to cars. There were no signs of unrest. Gregory was there.

Why were my emotions so strong and so deep at this moment? When I went back to Mississippi in 2006 and met with Simon's family members, I felt compelled to apologize.

It was genuine and heartfelt. Now, as I watched Charleston unfold, I desperately wanted someone with great authority, like our president, to seize this moment when we all felt so vulnerable and say those words on national TV. "I'm sorry. I'm so deeply sorry." Though the gesture could be seen as a paltry attempt to redeem us, it might steer us in the direction of healing. But now, when we needed it, our president couldn't entirely speak for white America. He could fulfill the role of Mourner in Chief but not deliver our national apology.

Where was Gregory during all of this historic activity? Doing his job. I knew not to distract him except to text something encouraging. There would be time to catch up after the city quieted down. I was able to read his Facebook posts. This one appeared on June 23rd:

> I remember the day I moved to SC from California. I saw that Confederate flag hanging high outside the state capitol. I said to myself "Damn I don't think i'm welcome here & it's going to be a long road living in Charleston." I must say I couldn't be happier that that flag will come down. It's just 1 less distraction (from the many that still need to be fixed) for natives & outsiders like me to feel the culture of the 1850s still lingering in SC in 2015. It's time to move upward & forward & that flag has no place in our future.

On July 10, the South Carolina legislature voted unanimously to remove the confederate flag from the state house in Columbia. This happened in the state that in 1860 was first to secede from the union and first to hear gunshots in the Civil War. In anticipation of unrest during the flag lowering ceremony, Governor Haley advised people to disregard the "disruptive hateful spectacle" of the KKK and "to make the statehouse a lonely place for them."

I spoke to the black deacon at my church, seeking her opinion. First, when I mentioned the flag, she said, "It's just a distraction from the real problems." I could understand her point and her cynicism. Removing the flag was not, in and of itself, going to change the racial climate in our country. Then we talked about the atrocity at Mother Emanuel in Charleston and the beautiful response at our St. James AME Church. The depth of her sacrifice to serve a mostly white congregation became clear when she responded to my thoughts about the difference in our churches. She said, "When confronted with racism, we haven't had anywhere to go except to our Lord. When you [white people] lose a job or can't get a loan or have a medical emergency, you can call on each other. We have no privilege, no advantages, nothing to do except take it to God." I heard her. Her honesty with me came from a respectful place, not angry, just honest.

For a few weeks to come, the lowering of the confederate flag was indeed a distraction. Ku Klux Klaners voiced their anger, saying, "They're taking our heritage from us. They're taking the freedom out of America." Plans were underway for a rally on July 19. Gregory made his apprehension known on Facebook. He wrote:

> I'm covering a KKK rally tomorrow they're upset the confederate flag is off the SC Statehouse & I can't sleep because I cant stop thinking about it. I've never met one, and i'm praying I stay cool. When I see the cone hats and start hearing White Supremacy jargon it will truly be a test to my faith for Christ said: "But I tell you,

love your enemies and pray for those who persecute you," Matthew 5:44 NIV

He received many supportive comments from friends and family. The national media didn't report the intensity of the atmosphere in Columbia. That was probably intentional, so as to tamp down some of the fire or at least keep it from spreading. But Gregory was there and this is what he reported:

Email dated July 21, 2015

Yea the real scene looked this. With snipers on roof of the statehouse, state and local police plus national guard on ground. The fights the arguing ppl pulling out knives some getting hit in head with bottles, it just got too real. It didn't feel like 2015, it felt jim crow civil rights south, except Black folk wasnt singing we shall overcome they were busting heads of any white supremacist they could find. They wasn't taken no mess. Everything went 0 to 100 real quick when the kkk arrived.

The white hot anger of the KKK wasn't snuffed out that day. Over the past two decades, arson in predominantly African American churches had declined, but in the first weeks after the removal of the flag, at least six congregations lost their spiritual homes to intentional fires.

I thought of all that Gregory had seen during his almost two year stint in Charleston. His time in the Deep South had been challenging, but one day he will think back on these history-making moments. His coming of age as a reporter brought out many character assets he may not have known he had when he moved into Mount Pleasant, South Carolina.

I called Pat on a Monday morning in August and found her cool headed and unconcerned. When I asked about how she thought Gregory was getting along, she referred to the topic of the flag. She said, "We're not living in the past. Think about the future." Perhaps living across the country in a place where people have a more liberal and accepting attitude freed Pat from a stronger reaction. "What bothers me," she continued, "is that we as a nation don't have to hold onto it…southern racists are from the old school. They're just trying to hold on."

Her attitude surprised me and gave me pause to think about my fear that intense emotion in American cities could escalate into more violence. An article in *The Guardian* by Max Blau quoted a senior fellow at the Southern Poverty Law Center. "…the KKK has fewer than 4,000 members, down from four million at its peak in the 1920s and roughly 40,000 members at the height of the civil rights movement in the 1960s." The Klan is ineffective now because of divisions in the ranks and poor leadership. Maybe Pat is right. Maybe the removal of the flag represented something more than a distraction. Maybe it was indicative of a more hopeful, peaceful time to come.

Chapter 13

LOOPS

Email dated August 26, 2015

> *I'm literally numb right now. Just thanking God i'll
> be home in a week or so my last day here is Friday.
> I need to be with my fam right now until I figure out
> my next move.*

NOW THAT I HAD ACCUMULATED SIXTY-SIX YEARS OF
life experience, and now that I was the mother of two grown
daughters and the grandmother of three beautiful small
people, I found it increasingly difficult to keep up with
the rapid pace of change that began with the "invention"
of social media. It seemed as if all of the rules of engage-
ment had changed, and though I had spent over twenty-
four years in classrooms teaching language and literature,
my complaints about modern media would not stop the
technology train or even slow it down. My children had
instructed me to quit writing long emails, stop calling them
for a catch-me-up talk. Texting, they said, was the best way
to communicate with them. I hated to text. My fingers were
too big for the miniature keyboard on the IPhone that they

gave me one Chrismas. Shortening words to their essential phonetic elements felt wrong but correct spelling was becoming an obsolete protocol.

In the summer of 2015 I fell ill with some intestinal malady that lasted six weeks. My internist put me through a battery of tests but no diagnosis could be made. Because I have an active imagination and the propensity to catastrophize, fear took over and I became certain that I had a terminal illness that would result in my demise within a fairly short span of time. I texted. "Not well. Lots of tests. No answers yet." This is the response I got: "Sorry u r going thru this." That's all. Privately I was hurt. When I complained to my friends, they didn't help. Rather they insisted that our young people are so busy and so inundated with information that I should not expect anything more than an occasional text.

A similar situation arose with Gregory. During and after the devastating incident at Mother Emanuel, Channel 4 overwhelmed him with assignments. He didn't read his email but relied on texting, twitter and Facebook. It seemed important for me to find out about his experience on the front line in Charleston during that time, and I knew his two year contract would soon end. I didn't want to lose touch with him. As instructed, I texted on and off for a couple of weeks with no response. At the same time, I was preoccupied with my health, became distracted and forgot to check Greg's Facebook entries. If I had, I would have discovered that he was leaving Channel 4 without a clear next step in his emerging career.

Finally, an email dinged into place on my desk top:

My nana asked me about you and made me realize

I completely forgot we were supposed to talk!! You have probably been calling my 843 number which I don't have anymore because I quit my job and moved back to CA. My personal number is _____.. Im not working so im pretty much always free. Ill be going to church in about an hr, other than that give me a ring!

Time…I thought. Give him some time. It was obvious to me that this young man had enough to do just to process his tenure in South Carolina. He had witnessed trauma and observed the effects of it. Had his experiences with it traumatized him in turn? We would have that conversation in time. I already knew from earlier communication that Gregory was not the same optimistic and naïve twenty-four year old that I met in L.A. in 2013.

Twenty-four. That was the age of my father when he returned to Mississippi after World War II. While flying warplanes in the Eastern Theatre of Operation, he had seen plenty of trauma as well. His service to our country put him in harm's way and taught him how to defend himself and end the lives of the enemy. He came back to the family plantation wanting nothing more than to reenter a world he knew and understood. That world was not just or fair but it was predictable. He had power and control, not to mention privilege and status, and he was once again surrounded by people he knew and loved, both black and white.

When Dad decided to quit farming and move into newspaper work, that decision may have been predicated on his sense that change was in the offing. He would have known that big farming was moving into plantation operations. Black workers that counted on their jobs would be replaced by massive combines, tractors, cultivators and planters.

The change that probably would have worried him most, however, was what he might have seen in the countenance of black farm workers. Some had recently returned from serving in WW II, like Simon. They might have felt empowered, but most certainly, by 1946, they would be chafing under the Jim Crow laws and the failure of emancipation to appreciably change their lives. Dad would have found out that his old friends, Charlie Lee Jr. and Charlie Lee Sr. and his wife, had picked up and moved to California. Attrition of blacks out of the South was on the rise. If this trend took on steam, who would do the physical labor?

Both Dad and Gregory stepped into their roles in journalism with the hopefulness and naivete of youth. The major difference was that Gregory left his family behind in California. His new life would render him completely isolated. He would see South Carolina erupt into a racial Armageddon. Dad reentered the fold with a wife and baby boy by his side. He was "back home" in safety and security. In both places there existed a long and troubling history of slavery.

For most of my life I have had to fight a kind of mental lethargy. Too easily I fall into dualistic thinking. When a dissonance or a divergence arises, it is very easy for me to go left or go right; to think black or to think white. What about gray? What about brown? It takes effort for me to hold contradictory evidence in my hands, giving ambiguity its due. In truth, ambiguity and even paradox when accepted, forge a space in which something positive can happen—change, understanding, forgiveness, love, sanity. For example, since I was a teen, the character of Atticus Finch from *To Kill a Mockingbird* has stood out in my mind as the ideal, honorable and Christ-like, yet flat example of the potential for goodness. Each year that I taught, my students read the story of Jean Louise Finch. I have seen the movie dozens of times. Prior to 2006 and the discovery of our family's dark, secret past, I could appreciate its picture of southern family life, and I could see or wanted to see Atticus in my father. I wanted to think that Dad, like Atticus, would stand up for the wrongfully accused, the oppressed, the poor and that he would do it with manners, grace and equanimity. I hung onto that idealized image of my father until I couldn't anymore.

But in July of 2015, a manuscript was discovered that was probably a first draft by Harper Lee. *Go Set a Watchman* was controversial from the start. Early reviews disclosed a frustrated readership. The portrayal of Atticus had taken a sharp right turn from the depiction of him in *To Kill a Mockingbird*. In this book he is bigoted, anti-integration, unempathetic and privileged. As I read the excitement and consternation in the posts of my friends on Facebook, I could feel a hard resistance building in me. I was not going to let Harper Lee or anyone else destroy my hero, and I stated as much in response to queries from fellow writers and friends. Atticus could be good or bad but he could not be both. I was not going to read the new Harper Lee novel.

Two weeks after the release, I stumbled on an opinion piece in the *New York Times* by Isabel Wilkerson, who I and others have found to be one of this generation's most powerful black voices. In "Our Racial Moment of Truth," I discovered the reason I had to reverse my decision about *Watchman*. She wrote,

> The importance of this new Atticus is that he is lay-
> ered and complex in his prejudices; he might even

be described as a gentleman bigot, well-meaning in his supremacy. In other words, he is human, and in line with emerging research into how racial bias has evolved in our society. He is a character study in the seeming contradiction that compassion and bigotry can not only reside in the same person but often do, which is what makes racial bias, as it has mutated through the generations, so hard to address.

These words settled on my heart like manna because I had—and I suspect many white people had—struggled with the pain of not being able to reconcile the good with the bad in their own and their forebears' natures. Here was a black historian saying, "Yes. It can."

About a year after Harper Lee's new book was published, I finally read it. Atticus is portrayal as a bigoted, narrow-minded 72 year old lawyer. Oddly, I found comfort in *Watchman*. Jean Louis experienced the same disillusion and disappointment that I had come to feel with regard to my father. Dad, like Atticus, was trapped in history. My job now is to love him despite his terribly flawed past.

Nonetheless, I have struggled with the notion that the racists in my family embody a dark, pernicious morality. I found it almost impossible to reconcile that with my memories from childhood of the caring, principled, loyal and good sides of the people I loved. My grandmother, for example, struggled to raise four small children and to run a plantation and a gin—by herself. At the same time, she was motherly and protective—not merely maternalistic and proprietary—of the black people who worked for her, even though she was exacting about the work that had to be done. One summer when I visited her, she took me along on one of her many trips to the Sharky County health clinic to check on the well-being of an injured worker. I heard numerous tales of her extraordinary efforts to get workers medical attention when they needed it. She was forced by circumstances to use her strength and exercise her will so as to survive after becoming a widow at the age of thirty-four. She didn't have time to consider options. The existing social order was what it was, and she had to find a way to work within it and around it. She was not an either/or person. She was both.

Fortunately for beleaguered Mat, Dad's cousin's family, the Hedges moved to the Delta to help and stayed for about five years. The year after they moved to Arkansas, Mamaw was a single mother. She carried on until her nest was empty and then began to import grandchildren during holidays and summers.

WHAT MADE IT SO HARD FOR ME TO RECONCILE THE goodness in my grandmother with her way of diminishing people of color was the same stuff that engendered bias and prejudice in me. Love.

Mamaw was sensitive to the deficits in my home life and to my overly sensitive nature. She made it her mission to protect and nurture all of her grandchildren until we developed inner resources and strength. For her, my birthright entitled me to certain advantages.

The ceiling fan in the sunroom at Greenfields is ticking out the minutes in the late afternoon. Mamaw is fresh from her nap, outfitted in a yellow linen dress with an oblong Victorian diamond broach, a gift from Thomas, pinned to her bosom. On the floor beside her, a rattan basket full of skeins of pastel yarn yield a single thread up to her lap and into dexterous hands. I'm nestled by her side watching her fingers fly while the thread turns into interlocking loops. A soon-to-be baby blanket.

"Here," she says, extracting a length of baby blue, "we start with a slip knot like this. Now practice making a chain of stitches by looping your hook through this link."

I followed her lead and soon had a messy chain of stitches syncopated by the occasional dropped loop.

She said, "It's okay but you must practice. Let's start over." I tried to interlock the stitches perfectly and when I had a good, solid chain, she showed me how to double back a second, interlinked loop. This way my creation grew both horizontally and vertically.

While I lapped up the warmth and comfort in her physical proximity, I was aware that Mat and Jo, dressed in starched pale gray uniforms, scurried about the house. Mat worked in the kitchen. She washed and parboiled vegetables plucked from the garden that very day. Maybe she fried chicken or roasted a tenderloin or kneaded bread dough. Jo, who had straightened and swept out the house, washed and ironed laundry, set the table while she mumbled about some grievance just shy of being audible. I was taught to be courteous and respectful but there was no confusion about my ascending rank in the household. They were servants. I was in the bloodline. The consistent orbit of that world depended on an inviolable hierarchy: Matt, Jo and others with different, specific jobs to do under the command of my Grandmother.

By this time, Mamaw's nest was completely empty so most summers she drove the 700 miles across three states to gather grandchildren. A pied piper if there ever was one. We spent two weeks at a time in the Delta. During the fall and winter months I looked forward to powder blue envelopes that arrived in the mail. Also during those non-planting months, Mamaw provided the black women with materials to make candlewick bedspreads. Aunt Mat and others were paid $6 a week for the products of their cottage industry.

When my brother, Jay, finished high school, my Fleming grandparents (Mom's) gifted him and one cousin with a Brownell tour of Europe. To insure that I had a similar experience, Mamaw paid a visit to Mom's parents and offered to chaperone a similar tour for me and the sons of four family friends on the condition that they pay my way. She devised a plan to visit seven countries in five weeks. Not long after high school graduation, we sailed out of New York on the Queen Elizabeth for France. Because of her largess I experienced cultures I would not have known: major museums, restaurants, theatres, antiquities and music venues. That trip expanded my thinking as much or more than the ensuing four years of college.

Few of my friends were privy to the wedding gift that Mamaw spent months preparing before my wedding. I was too shy and naïve to think they would appreciate my trousseau. It was just something I thought too dated to share. A large box arrived from Anguilla with my name on it. Inside I found sets of sheets embellished with lace, bath towels with hand embroidery, kitchen towels (some of which I still use today). Her handiwork was intended to set my union off on the right foot, the proper and appropriate foot.

ON OCTOBER 4, 2015, AT THE HOME OF HIS MOTHER Latoya, I caught up with Gregory. When he first spoke, I wasn't sure I had the right person on the other end of the phone. The voice sounded deeper, less enthusiastic, tired but not emotional. It was a voice gone flat, coming from a person who was deflated and numb. Immediately I felt sorry for the call and wished I could just hang up the phone.

I asked Gregory where he was when he heard about the shootings at Mother Emanuel. Before he started to tell me his story he said that he had been involved in a different congregation in Charleston, but through his job he had come to know Rev. Pinckney whom he had interviewed and befriended. Gregory would have known that after the death of Walter Scott, Clemente Pinckney, a state senator since the age of twenty-three, was helping to get a bill through the legislature that would require police officers to wear body cameras. Pinckney had invited Gregory to go with him to his A.M.E. church near downtown. Greg wasn't able to follow through until after the shootings. He said, "I was sad that my first time attending a service wasn't because he asked me to…But because I was assigned to cover his funeral."

When he got the call from his station manager, "All I could think about is that it could have been me." I took a deep breath until he could continue.

"I had just got off work, and I was on my way home. I took a shower and ate dinner. When I got out of the shower I had missed three calls, maybe more. I called my boss and said , "Hey, what's going on." She said to come to the station right away. Someone just shot up a church. During the weeks immediately following those phone calls, he was sent hither and yon reporting. When President Obama arrived in town for the funeral of Clemente Pinckney, Greg was on the street interviewing people who were turned away from the arena, even after spending hours in line to get in.

He told me that the community was still healing from the Walter Scott incident when Dylann Roof opened fire. More than once, Greg talked about the heated racial climate and how it affected him and his co-workers. He was "almost jumped," and a friend was hit in the head with a bottle. Another co-worker had his camera smashed.

When he covered the KKK rally and the subsequent removal of the Confederate Flag from the state house, he said he was "called the N word three times." He was booed. He was mooned. Someone said, "Go back to Africa." When I told him that I was relieved that he was at last home with his folks, he said in the weariest of tones, "I just got so numb to all those murders." At that moment, I wished that I hadn't pressed him to talk about his experience. I couldn't think of any way to elevate his mood. Stupidly, I continued.

"Greg, some writers and speakers are saying that Charleston was and is a turning point in our race war. Did you see any evidence of change for good?"

I thought that maybe the removal of the flag was a promising sign to him.

All he could say was, "I don't know. I just don't know. Living in the trenches you see a lot of the evil that still exists. I had to leave a live shot because I was afraid for my life. In those moments you see the extremes on both sides. Yes, there was an outpouring of love. There was also evil."

While Greg was going through this, Latoya was well aware of the challenges her son was facing on the job. On July 21st, she wrote the following Facebook post:

Of course my son had to cover the KKK rally over the weekend in SC. The news story here is very watered down for television. Believe me when I say racism and

the white supremacy movement has gained momen-
tum. They are no longer hiding behind sheets. And for
those of you who feel we should just "move on", tell
that to my son who just a few days ago was referred
to several times as "nigga" "boy" and told to "go back
to Africa". Trust me I would love to move forward but
there is still much work to do.

Molly Walling

Chapter 14

"WE ARE NOT RACIST."

—————⟨∞⟩—————

1970. In my sophomore year at Converse College, an all-women's school, I fell in love with a neighbor and friend from back home, one that I'd known since high school. He was witty, brilliant, and I loved his parents. The following year I traveled to the University of Virginia by any form of transportation I could find, even the Greyhound bus, which took twice as long to get to Charlottesville as did a car, such was my enthusiasm for our relationship and its potential. Once together, our talk was all counterculture. We went to hear Jefferson Airplane perform on the steps of the Rotunda at Mr. Jefferson's university. We protested, and we partied hard. He graduated a year ahead of me, and several weeks after he tossed his tasseled cap into the air, we were married.

The plan was for my new husband to go to law school at UVa, but he would have to wait a year to matriculate because of his draft status and my need to finish my last semester of college. We drove to Spartanburg that summer, found an apartment on Main Street within walking distance of Converse and a teaching position for him in the public school system. Fortunately, since we were pacifists, the draft lottery ended before his number so he was not required to go to Viet Nam. We celebrated that good luck with a bottle of champagne.

According to the South Carolina Public Library archives, the school where my now ex-husband was hired to teach math, was "opened in 1926 for African American students in grades one through nine. Later, grades ten and eleven were added. The school closed in 1969 after court-ordered integration." But that is not accurate. It remained open for at least one more year, the first of integration. Every day, when I left to walk to class, he was already on his way to his students.

He told me about the frustrations of working with these sixth graders. "I've got a fifteen-year-old in my class with eleven and twelve year olds." Some students were able to multiply and divide. Others were only skilled at addition and subtraction. They were mostly black, poor, and sometimes hungry. When they went to the lunchroom, he stayed behind eating a sandwich and reading in the classroom. Some days, the sandwich I'd packed for his lunch became sustenance for a student. As I expected, he was able to keep them engaged in learning by spiking their lessons with a full jigger of humor. By Christmas, his frustration had subsided, and I surmised that he had become invested in "his" kids and they in him. He told me he loved them.

Then, the awful day came.

"You won't believe what happened to Junior."

His voice was raspy with anger and hurt. I thought perhaps a child had been seriously injured or even died. "Tell me."

"Walking to school this morning, Junior and his friends were minding their own business when they heard tires screeching around the corner behind them. The next thing they knew, a carload of high school or college students slowed down just long enough to throw a bag of urine at the kids." His fists clenched and his voice wavered—two things I had not seen my new husband do because he kept his emotions under tight wrap.

I stood perfectly still as he described Junior's appearance and tears. My husband may have told me that he had never seen anything so awful. He may have expressed a desire to do something about it. One thing is for certain, he never forgot that incident. It was as if he, himself, had been a target.

Throughout the duration of our thirty year marriage, I never heard him make an unkind remark about a person of color. Sometimes when we gathered with other young married couples for drinks, the men hovered in one corner of the room and the "nigger" jokes started. Every man present laughed except one. My husband didn't step up to oppose the defamation of an entire race of people—not in social settings anyway. He was more likely to quietly slip from the room to refill his glass or get something to eat.

Because of his and my refusal to make derogatory comments about blacks, our daughters expressed surprise when I first told them my family's story and my plans to write about it. Our oldest said, "Mom, we are not racist. Neither you nor dad say anything negative about black people." She was right. We didn't talk about racial issues at all. It is fair to say that this failing of ours was one we shared with many white families that considered themselves liberal. We didn't teach our daughters how the privileges of being born white had afforded them a life like very few African Americans would ever know. At that time, my focus for my children was on giving them every possible advantage. I was blind about how easy it was for me to do that compared to the good folks who lived in the housing projects.

What I didn't tell my children about being born white begins with my family of origin. Even though there had been significant racial prejudice and violence unknown to me until after my children were grown, I was not taught to see it in systems but rather in individual acts. That black kids in our schools, for example, were oftentimes considered underachievers was a reflection on them, not on the education system.

I should have explained that in cities with a larger black population, people often chose the houses they lived in based on location and the assurance that their property values would not be affected by the color of their neighbor's skin. They could make that choice knowing that they could afford to live there, and get a loan from the bank without concern that their financial reliability would be judged by their color. Their neighbors would be "trustworthy" and pleasant to them.

Our family moved into an area with public schools but chose to educate our children in private ones. We knew but didn't think about the fact that they would learn about their race and little, if anything, about others. I didn't have to teach my Caucasian children that they would have to be especially vigilant about who might object to them because of their race, who might do them physical harm, who might judge them.

I didn't have to explain to them that the police wouldn't necessarily protect them, might in fact single them out and discount their story. I wouldn't have to caution them that people in authority of another race have power over them so they must be fearful and extra cautious when outside their home; that that might result in not being as well cared for by legal or medical persons.

I didn't have to tell them that they would have to work harder to get the same job as a white person. That they might not earn as much for the same work so it would be hard to save and move up in society. The American Dream of getting educated, getting a good job, buying a house, getting married and starting a family has been an ideal largely attainable for whites only. Hard work for blacks might not pay them enough to even maintain their position.

And perhaps most important of all, because black Americans are disrespected outside their homes by so many, they could easily feel rejection and shame and lack of worth. Those feelings of being undervalued, when turned inward, can overshadow the gifts, the potential and the promise of personal growth and expression so that people can become stunted and fail to thrive.

I didn't tell my children that if these things could change, it would make their own lives so much better.

THE SCHOOL WHERE MY HUSBAND TAUGHT IS NOT listed on the Fisk University data-base of Rosenwald Schools, as is the Anguilla School built in 1921-22, in Sharkey County, Mississippi, where my family lived. Due to the largess of Julius Rosenwald, 633 schools were built in Mississippi alone. He was a wealthy clothier who later became part owner and CEO of Sears Roebuck, and he had the heart and vision to create a fund that would help to alleviate the disparity in education for black children throughout the south during the early years of the twentieth century. From 1896 until the 1910s, the mandate of Plessy

v. Ferguson, which required that separate schools for the races must provide equal opportunity, went largely ignored. Rosenwald must have known that the policy wasn't being enforced because school boards were made up of whites who funneled monies into white schools.

Julius partnered with the Tuskegee Institute after he met Booker T. Washington. Together they established a cooperative agreement with communities where the schools were built. Thus the beginnings of "the matching grant." For example, the Anguilla School cost a total of $3600. Rosenwald provided $1200, the public provided $1200 and local African Americans provided $1200. The schools were built according to two plans, both of which incorporated electricity and adequate ventilation. In some locations, communities who could not contribute financially were funded on a commitment of labor.

Rosenwald was Jewish. His affinity for blacks and compassion for them due to the persecution they experienced in our country made for a beneficial liaison with people who desperately sought to elevate themselves through education. The willingness of the black citizens to do the hands-on work of building the schools is a testament to their longing and determination.

Charlie Lee Jr. entered the first grade in 1936 at the Anguilla School; Virginia followed him in 1938. It is safe to speculate that they at least noticed each other while in school. We know that for many children, attendance was affected by the cycles of the planting season. At harvest time, they would be out in the fields working alongside their parents. Many children stopped going to school altogether after fourth grade. By then they would have benefited from a curriculum that focused on vocational training.

According to the *Mississippi History Now* journal, most of the lessons revolved around learning agricultural skills and mechanical training.

Simon's mother, Leana, cared for Virginia and kept her in her home on the Hall Plantation. At some point, probably when Charlie Lee was in his late teens, he "took a shine" to Virginia, slipped out from under Aunt Mat and made his way to Dr. Hall's place to see her. Their clandestine meetings in Leana's house resulted in their first pregnancy when Virginia was not yet fifteen.

The roles of Leana and Mat in the shaping of the lives of these two young people cannot be stressed enough. Their fathers were absent during Virginia's and Charlie Lee's formative adolescent years. Simon had enlisted and Charlie Lee Sr. had relocated to southern California. This dynamic was endemic in black families in the states then and it still is. Though I never met Leana, Aunt Mat made a strong impression on me. She was quiet, respectful, dignified in her demeanor and in her actions. She spoke few words but they were weighted, so I respected her in turn. I knew that when I was in her presence, I was safe. Children see into the hearts of other people. They are not tripped up by superficial differences like skin color. My siblings and cousins knew beyond question that Aunt Mat was not to be trifled with or there would be unpleasant consequences. Even my grandmother whose "superiority" over Mat was sanctioned by the social order of her day, would not question Aunt Mat's judgment. If she reported on us for misbehavior, we would suffer every time, so I know how important her presence was in Charlie Lee's youth and in my father's.

Nonetheless, there was a time when I was naïve enough to think that Mat's comportment was required of her by

Mamaw. Now I know that Aunt Mat had an innate morality that was sufficient unto itself. She needed no training from Mamaw and she was not alone. I was unaware that there existed a code of decorum within the black community that was based on the cultivation of respectability as a means of gaining ground on civil rights. As early as 1898, The National Association of Colored Women had been established with Mary Church Terrell at its helm. She gave a speech to another women's group that year and said,

> Through mothers' meetings, which are a special feature of the work planned by the Association, much useful information in everything pertaining to the home will be disseminated. ... The more unfavorable the environments of children, the more necessary is it that steps be taken to counteract baleful influences on innocent victims. How imperative is it then that as colored women, we inculcate correct principles and set good examples for our own youth, whose little feet will have so many thorny paths of prejudice, temptation, and injustice to tread.

Though I have no way of knowing whether the NACW was organized in the Delta, Mat and Leana were probably made aware of these efforts.

In the October 2015 issue of *Harper's Magazine*, Randall Kennedy, black Professor at Harvard Law School, addresses the efficacy of "respectability politics." While I'm aware that his hypothesis is controversial, I find it useful in this context.

"My parents sternly ordered their children to be dignified in the presence of white people so that there would be no opportunity to put us in racist, stereo-typical categories."

Kennedy's stern upbringing had dual purposes. First, his own parents sought to make their children less vulnerable to white aggression. They not only wanted their children to remain alive but also to develop into responsible adults and flourish.

Another aspect of "respectability" comes from the teachings of women like Mary Church Terrell: that black people could be physically restrained, but their inner life was neither accessible to whites nor was it malleable. That is, they could be outwardly demeaned and downtrodden, but ultimately they had control of their own thoughts and reactions. Thus, efforts to elevate their status by purity of thought, manner, speech and appearance would not only advance them, and improve the perception of reliability but would, Kennedy suggests, "reinforce their sense of moral superiority over whites." What Aunt Mat, Leana and others inculcated in the minds of their children, grandchildren and the white children they served was, essentially, a moral high ground, which ultimately fed a sense of hope and maybe even more important, the ability to be resilient. By being realistic about racism and by investing in themselves, young blacks were able to envision a positive future for themselves and work toward it. They could reach down and lift up the next generation. Their deportment had the potential to engender respect in whites.

WHAT HAD HAPPENED TO GREGORY SINCE I LAST spoke with him? Where was he and how had he fared during and after the nightmare of Mother Emanuel where nine innocent people died in Charleston? For a young, idealistic man starting his career in journalism, the racial events that had taken place in Charleston during his tenure there would surely have disillusioned if not traumatized him.

Soon after the incident, I wrote to Latoya, Gregory's mother, and asked about him. She responded that he was in L.A. again, adjusting and enjoying a slower paced life outside of journalism until he procured another position. She encouraged me to call him. I also spoke with Pat, knowing that Gregory would be eager to spend time with his Nana. She confirmed that he was exhausted. He'd left South Carolina without a contract but with an impressive resume. Her advice to him was, "You're not going to lose. Things are better than what you expected. Stay positive. This time is here for a reason." Gregory's close relationship with Pat over his lifetime had influenced him in concrete ways. Her mantra when he called her, frustrated and overwhelmed, was this: "Good things and bad things will happen. Be thankful for all of it. That's how you learn." Her self-appointed job of lifting up other people, of being sensitive and responsive to the needs of others, must have been exhausting at times.

Gregory has his own Aunt Mat in Pat, who has always been able to reach down and grab her grandson. Her own grandfather's wife, Mama Lilly, taught her how to be the one who lifts others. Many family members have received the care that only Pat can give them. Virginia, for example, probably would have been equipped to succeed in the world if not for her father's death. Today Virginia's family members, including Greg, are doing fine in spite of what happened to her.

I asked Pat if she could think of what she learned from her own mother. She said, "Mama was stressed when we were growing up. She was an emotional young mother because of her father. We watched out for her. When she was sober, she made sure we had our lunch made before we left for school." Was Virginia resilient? No. But she has had the good fortune to have a daughter who cares for her every day, providing three meals, baths, reading material and the occasional cigarette or glass of wine. Now, in the Fall of 2015, Virginia sleeps late into the morning. Pat fears that she won't wake up. When I asked how Virginia was getting along she said, "She's doing great. If she passed tomorrow, I'll know that she was happy."

Was Greg going to be resilient after Charleston? Absolutely. Pat was eager to tell me that he had been offered a job in Fresno with KSEE 24/CBS47 and Telemundo. In the few months since his return to California, he had rented and moved into an apartment and was working hard. Most important to her was the fact that Greg was the first black reporter/anchor on a Spanish news station. Fluent in Spanish, after spending a year in the Dominican Republic during his college years at Clark Atlanta University, he can now use his language skills to bring unfolding events to Latinos living in the valley.

September 2015. Feeding frenzy. Rhythm and Blues singer, Patti Labelle, aged 71, contracted with Walmart to sell her sweet potato- "Patti Pies." The country went wild and Walmart sold on average one pie per second for days, if not weeks. On November 11, as I was cranking through my Facebook Wall posts, a video brought me to a full-on halt. With her video camera Latoya captured a happy, smiling Greg in her kitchen, seated on a stool with a pie slicer in his hand, and two "Beulah Mae" pies resting on a cooling rack in the foreground. He said he'd got word that Latoya was making her "mama pies" while he was shopping at

Walmart. He left the store and drove straight to her house. In the video, he picked up a pie, smelled it, indicated that the aroma was mind-blowing, and then sliced into the pumpkin colored confection. He took his time guiding a forkful to his mouth. He chewed. His eyes rolled back in his head. His smile grew wider. And then… he jumped off the stool and danced a little jitterbug about the kitchen to the howling laughter of Latoya and Pat.

I knew then that he was going to be okay.

Chapter 15

DNA

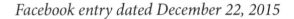

Facebook entry dated December 22, 2015

Sometimes I wonder what country in Africa would I be
from & what my life would be like if slavery never happened #ThinkingOutLoud

MORE LIKELY THAN NOT, GREGORY'S ANCESTORS HAD
been slaves who might have come through Charleston's
historic port of entry. Now, three years after we met, he
has removed himself from the Deep South. His stint of
reporting from the city that witnessed the intake of more
slaves than any other in the U.S. is over. From California to
Charleston, "ground zero for the history of slavery," according to Charleston commentator Brian Hicks, Greg made it
half way back to Africa and now—home again.

Dr. Darren Waters, black Professor of History at UNC
Asheville, speaks publicly about the status of racism in our
city and says, "What is at the heart of the African American experience is slavery. It is very hard to look at how
bad it was. We dance around slavery because it was just
too awful." In 1670, Charleston was founded and named

Charlestown. By 1698 it was the center of the slave trade in North America, and for about 200 years the city thrived on a slave economy. Not surprisingly, the first shots fired in the Civil War were heard in Charleston, as current residents proudly inform tourists.

The convergence of the Ashley and Cooper Rivers made for a harbor easily accessible to ships. Forty percent of enslaved Africans were brought in via the Charleston Harbor. Once on solid ground, they were cleaned up and fed—just like calves made ready for the market place. The reason for such an influx into the Low Country can be summed up in one word: rice. South Carolina's primary cash crop, it required ten times the labor needed to harvest cotton. Africans had been rice growers for thousands of years. They fit the profile Low Country planters were looking for, but fieldwork was not the sum total of their working life. Some also labored in other trades like brick making, horse grooming, domestic help and carpentry. Because it was common for slave women to suffer sexual exploitation at the hands of their owners, there is now a major ethnic sub-group of bi-racial individuals in and around Charleston and elsewhere.

On April 10, 2011, the Charleston *Post and Courier* carried an article by Brian Hicks, entitled "Slavery in Charleston: A Chronology of Human Bondage in the Holy City."

> Most of these slaves lived in cabins on the planta-
> tion grounds, small shacks that generally held ten
> or more people. They made their clothes from cloth
> provided by their owners once a year, usually at
> Christmas. Also, they were given a pair of shoes
> meant to last an entire year but... most slaves would

wear out footwear within a few months of work. By summer, most were working barefoot in the fields.

Living conditions were dire but even worse was the brutal physical abuse that many of their overseers and bosses utilized to maintain control and increase productivity. Coded in the DNA of many black Americans living today is the cellular memory of brutality—pain and the scarring of bodies, hearts and souls.

For Gregory, spending almost two years in Charleston as a fledgling reporter triggered some deeply rooted responses to the inhumanity and violent behavior of whites toward people of color for hundreds of years. On the day the confederate flag was removed from the state capital, Gregory was reporting there. He witnessed the hatred of the KKK, the vestiges of the worst of the slave culture. No wonder he fled back to California in a dead heat. But not even a new job, in familiar territory, settling back into an environment more liberal and ethnically diverse, could keep him from glancing over his shoulder at Charleston or from hearing a distant call from the shores of West Africa.

During my first visit to California to meet Gregory and his family at Pat's house, his mother Latoya expressed an interest in pursuing that unresolved question that surfaced during my *Death in the Delta* research, the whispers of a genetic connection piqued her interest. By that time I had an account with Ancestry.com and was using the site to build out my family tree and to access historic records of my people and Simon's.

When I returned to Asheville from California, the idea of going deeper in my investigation led me to consider our options for finding genetic connections. Since Virginia was

Simon's closest living relative, she would be the obvious choice for DNA testing. Not only did I have serious questions about how my family would react to any pursuit of this nature, I wasn't sure what it would mean to me or to Virginia. Was it feasible, even ethical, to solicit her involvement? Now 83 years old, bedridden and housebound, she might resist or find it intrusive. Was I taking advantage of her when she had already been victimized by my family? Would she rather not know? Did she even care? What lay ahead of me was a quagmire of emotions and a process so frustrating that I almost gave up. Communication with the California contingency, 2300 miles away, bogged down and almost ground to a halt.

The reasons for this were numerous. When Gregory was in Charleston he was unable to devote any time to the project. Latoya spent eight or more hours a day at her job. She lived over an hour away from Pat, who was adept at texting but still didn't have a computer. I had to depend on the postal service and the phone to reach her. I would have to put into writing the directions she needed to administer the test to Virginia. Then Latoya would have to be the conduit between me, her family and Ancestry.

Though I had been to see the Toombs family in California three times and Pat and I had forged a strong friendship based on kindred sentiments, it was difficult to slow her down during a conversation. She jumped from topic to topic with lightning speed, always passionate, always open to my input. How was I going to help her follow the protocol for any sort of DNA test? She, like me, knew from watching TV that we just needed a swab of saliva. That would have been easily accomplished, but it wasn't that simple.

Finding a testing center was another thorny issue. I was aware of the company, 23&Me based out of Mountain View, California. Right about the time I was prepared to push forward, the Federal Drug Administration shut down the genome service due to failure to comply with regulations. That was in 2013. In February of that same year Ancestry.com had made DNA testing a part of their program. I ordered a kit on line and sent it to Pat with instructions. She would need to remove the small vial with the black line on its side indicating filling amount. Virginia would have to gather enough sputum to spit into the vial. Then Pat would secure the cap and return the vial in its original packaging to Ancestry. It would take between four and six weeks to get the results. Latoya would need the activation code printed on the inside of the box so that she could access the DNA information on her computer.

I waited and waited. Month after month passed without any word from Latoya. Finally I was notified by Ancestry that the sample had failed to produce results. When I called Pat to tell her, she said that Virginia had been smoking prior to collection, and that Pat had given her a sugar drink to activate her salivary glands. No wonder the test failed, but it was partly my fault. A warning about not smoking or drinking for an hour prior to the test was right there on the package. I didn't make Pat sufficiently aware.

DURING THE ENSUING MONTHS, MY MOTHER'S health began its final decline. My sister and I moved her from her home to an assisted living apartment to a nursing facility and then on April 23, 2014, she left us. Fortunately, her mental stability hadn't completely flat-lined. I was able sit with her for long hours and chat about whatever surfaced in her mind. We took care of unfinished business between us and said those important words to each other again and again… I love you. When she died, she didn't know that my book had been published. It was best to let rest a subject so distressing to her.

Shortly after Mom's funeral, a new DNA kit arrived in the mail. This time, I sat down and wrote the directions out very clearly and posted it to California. Pat, as I came to understand, had total command when it came to her mother. She told Virginia that we needed another sample and she complied without resistance. It seemed that at last we would have an answer, but I continued to feel mixed emotions. The prevailing feeling had its genesis in shame. Over the course of the previous two years, I had come to care very deeply for Gregory, Pat, Virginia and Latoya. My understanding of the challenges in their lives had made me more acutely aware of the dynamics of racism. I had grown up with all of the advantages of being white. Regardless of my station in life, I could not escape the reality that someone, many someones, had suffered so that I could live free and prosper. Gnawing at my subconscious was a feeling akin to "survivor's guilt." Then, when I found out that my father had taken the lives of two black men, that guilt increased into a sense of deep shame. I didn't want to drag Virginia's family down by association with me and my family. I was afraid that in my DNA and possibly in our joint DNA there exists a "killer" gene. Facing this reality made a big part of me want to take cover underneath the bed. But there was no going back now.

Furthermore, if Dad and his brothers had a motive for the shootings and if that motive had been to commit fratricide, to get rid of the possibility that they might have had a fellow inheritor, then Simon's death would have been a crime of much greater proportions. Since I hadn't found any evidence to corroborate a genetic connection, I'd been able to hold out hope that it wasn't true.

While I waited to hear the results of the new test, I checked my own DNA. In about a month, I got word that my test could be activated. Poring over the web page of my profile, I discovered more about my bloodline, but the pages and pages of results were difficult to navigate. The site estimated my ethnicity to be 79% British Isles, 7% Scandinavian, 4% Irish with traces of ancestry in other parts of Europe. Somehow learning this added to my sense of identity, and affirmed the strength of my connection to my family members. The site could give me access to other people's results, but I had to gain entrance to Virginia's page through Latoya.

The book in your hands seemed to hinge on the genetic connection between me and Virginia. For me and I expect, for many of my readers, the discovery through our DNA had the potential to bind Simon's and my family irrevocably together. This was the climax to which I would build my story arc. The months of not knowing had only served to intensify my angst about discovering the truth. I felt a heavy cloak of responsibility on my shoulders, but I couldn't articulate why it felt so important. Either we were related or we were not. I knew that the relationship forged between Pat and me was as close to sisterhood as possible. All we would need to do would be to nurture it. When I felt that there had been ample time to get Virginia's results, early in the winter of 2015, I picked up the phone and called Pat.

"Molly, Latoya has the code to activate the test. I'll ask her to call you." Those were Pat's words and barring another false test result, I trusted her and relaxed. But the question that continued to surface in my mind was this: Why hadn't Latoya called me already? What was on her mind? Though she had instigated the search, she seemed to be procrastinating now that we could finally know.

Throughout the winter and early spring of 2015, Latoya's Facebook posts focused on the flurry of police shootings of unarmed black men. She was proud that Greg was reporting on those events but also intensely angry that there was so much wanton killing. Reading her posts offered me the opportunity to witness her passionate responses. Over time I began to see a shift in her position from raw emotion to activism. She was clearly working out a plan to build community and make a difference in the lives of young black girls. Around the 4th of May, the following post appeared:

Gyrl Talk Awareness Brunch
Enjoy a fun, Mother-Daughter event designed to open communication and increase awareness of tough issues our girls are faced with today. Guest Speakers will share expert knowledge in the topics of Domestic Violence and Teens and Sex Trafficking. Material is appropriate for attendees ages 12 and up…

Gyrls 2 Gems Inc, located in Moreno Valley, California, is a youth confidence building program targeted for girls ages 8 and up. In addition to building confidence, the program is designed to open communication between Mother/Caretaker and child, improve relationships, cultivate good decision making, and tackle peer-pressure through interactive small group workshops.

Latoya had been busy! She had shelved the DNA project for matters of larger concern, ones that had the potential to make a difference in her world. I wrote her to find out if there was a way for me to advance her cause. At the end of the message, I asked if she'd heard from Ancestry. I wrote, "Your silence about that makes me think there is not a connection but we **are** connected whether or not it's in our DNA."

Email dated May 4, 2015

Oh my goodness. I forgot to follow up with you. So sorry. Please call me.

Wait. She forgot? Had I misread her initial enthusiasm? When we finally talked, she said again that she'd simply forgotten to connect with me. With a quieter voice she said she didn't see any genetic connections in the results. A few seconds of silence followed. I didn't know how to respond to her. My mind was shifting back to the story, now merely an unfounded rumor, that Simon was my Grandfather's "other" son. Now I would have to tease out that part of the family secret and look with fresh eyes at what remained.

Latoya finally spoke. "I wanted to stick with the story that we are related because there are so many parallels in our lives. I didn't want to believe the DNA results." At the end of this labyrinthine process, these words might have made me feel that it was all folly. I could have felt disappointed, as Latoya clearly did. But my initial reaction, after a deep breath, was to open up to a larger, more valuable realization. When I took into account the strength of the connection we had developed since Gregory first reached out to me, I became full of wonder and gratitude that it was possible for me, Virginia, Pat, Gregory and Latoya to have entered into such a sweet, caring and respectful relationship with each other. Shared genes could not have been more precious than that.

I thought back to the day we met, how Pat had opened her arms to me and taken me into her home, how we had bonded instantly. I thought about our long walk along the Pacific Ocean near Hermosa Beach, giddy as teenagers, the shared stories, the loving attention she paid to Virginia, who was the glue that bound our histories together. I thought of the long phone calls and how Pat, every time, encouraged me to keep in touch, "Call anytime." And with special fondness, I thought of the afternoon of my last visit when we spread out the contents of a file that contained Virginia's writings. Pouring over the paperwork, we sat across the table from each other, our heads nearly touching, leaning in and marveling at the evidence of Virginia's deep inner life, her love of her children, her struggles with depression, her faith.

Before we hung up, Latoya gave me the code for Virginia's test results. I made note of her ethnicity make-up, not knowing that once again I would be able to provide family information to Gregory. But first, I would follow through with my plan to verify the data from Ancestry.com. On June 5, 2015, I met with a geneticist from Mission Hospital in Asheville. I had copied the files from Virginia's and my DNA reports and sent them to Shearon Roberts, Genetic Counselor. When I first contacted her, she'd expressed curiosity about what markers Ancestry had used. She said, "My gut feeling is that the two of you are really not related because you would be related fairly closely in a genetic sense." So, if my Grandfather had been Simon's father, the markers would have strongly indicated that. When Shearon and I sat down for coffee at the Atlanta Bread Company, she verified that there was, in fact, no genetic relationship between me and Virginia. What I felt then and still feel is that the DNA results provided us with information. That was all. It didn't affect the emotional connection we had forged. We shared a story, a story as old as time, but we were writing a new and beautiful ending full of hope and truth and reconciliation.

Gregory's Facebook post dated
December 21, 2015

Sometimes I wonder what country in Africa would I be from & what my life would be like if slavery never happened #ThinkingOutLoud

I responded.

Greg, According to Virginia's DNA, your ancestors came from the west coast of Africa - 43% from Ivory Coast/ Ghana, 17% Nigeria, 14% Cameroon/Congo, 7 % Senegal. Of course these are just estimates. Your mom can help you access that site.

12/22/2015 2:16PM

Molly you are the biggest blessing EVER!
This is the best Christmas Gift i've ever received.

Chapter 16

IN WHITE FAMILIES

———⟨⟨⟨⟨⟩⟩⟩⟩———

I WOULD BE DISINGENUOUS IF I CLAIMED TO HAVE BEEN unaware that I might create a fracture in my family by exposing our family secret. But I can say with candor that I did not have the intention of hurting anyone. As this story came to light over the many years of investigation, I felt that my role was to give it voice. It seemed to live and breathe all on its own and to be part of some plan far beyond my capacity to imagine. In an oft quoted episode Detective Friday of Dragnet said, "All we know are the facts, ma'am." Some of the facts, in this old case, were indeterminate, but I trusted my reader to come to a logical conclusion. Part of me hoped that my family had reached a point, after sixty plus years, where we could talk about our shared history and the living legacy of our forebears. I was wrong.

"How did your family react to *Death in the Delta*?" This question comes up in every reading I present and every creative nonfiction class I teach. My initial reaction, one that I can't act upon, is to tell my audience to consult one of the fine texts about this genre for advice about the perils of writing about family. Because these stories can place the truthful writer directly in the crosshairs of contrasting family perceptions of what "really happened," I don't want to discourage people who themselves are willing to travel back in time, willing to look deeply inside for answers. Exposing my family's secret opened a chasm in the ground beneath my feet. It represented our family's fall from grace. Some could accept it; others could not. I still feel the burn of rejection. I hope the passage of time will soften the effects of disclosure on my family.

Several months before *Death in the Delta* was printed, I wrote a letter to my cousins. My intention was to give them a heads-up that parts of the narrative might be uncomfortable for them. I apologized in advance. They responded with a lengthy letter of which the following paragraphs were a part.

> *Although we can appreciate that your intention in writing this book was to find some understanding (and perhaps resolution) into the complexity of your father and the relationship you had with him, unfortunately you have done this without regard or respect for the impact this book would have on the other members of your family. Mississippi is our home; Sharkey County is where our parents chose to live, it is where we were raised, spent innumerable years of our lives, and have established long-standing relationships; we are the ones pursuing personal and professional lives in this area that will be affected by your "story"; and this book is being published and marketed here in Mississippi...which I am certain is not without design and forethought on your part. If you sense any bitterness in my response it is because I resent the effects that I have already witnessed your story having on my mother, my sisters, and me ...not to mention the effects that will be felt by the children*

*and grandchildren of my family, yet untold. I only
wish that you had heeded the advice of the MANY
people that urged you not to revisit and revive a
tragedy that inflicted much pain and sorrow then
and will undoubtedly bring much additional pain
and sorrow to many undeserving people now... both
in our family and the families of the two men killed
that night. It is just all so unnecessary!*

In this tier of the family hierarchy, I am still a pariah. Since
Death in the Delta was published, only three of my twelve
cousins have corresponded with me. Even more distressing
is the response of some in my immediate family. You may ask
why I dredge this up now, when the dust has at last begun to
settle on *Death in the Delta*. The nature of their response is
symptomatic of the tenacious grip of the mythos that families embrace and guard with steadfast care. When stories are
kept secret for generations in an effort to protect that mythos,
those stories don't simply go away because we don't want to
acknowledge them. They hide out in our vascular systems
and those of our off-spring. They have the potential to play
havoc with our subconscious lives. When any component
of those stories produces guilt, unacknowledged but present,
the mythos becomes even more firmly held.

I share this facet of the story not out of self-pity, but
because I feel strongly that the roots underneath the thorny
vegetation called racism are more deeply entrenched than
we want to acknowledge. But it is important to note that I
have a thick file of letters from readers who had a positive
response to the first book. Though "Shoot the Messenger"
seems to apply to me as author, I have surfaced from this
family drama with a full measure of hope.

My love for family has not diminished during the past ten years, it has grown, become real and true and unabashedly proud. Writing about what happened forced me to take off ill-fitting clothes and step out from behind a façade of respectability and privilege. Doing so allowed me to be more human, to be myself and to have compassion for all people who suffer oppression. It set me free.

In the course of my life I've come to know the broad spectrum of emotions, the prickly, potent, angry, painful feelings embedded in human experience. My father used to say that according to God's plan, all people suffer the same amount while they travel from womb to grave. It's just that adversity comes to us in different forms. To say that Dad's view has confused and challenged me is an understatement. Everywhere I go, I see people who are wired to cope, or to deny, or to somehow lah-de-dah their way out of suffering, especially suffering with and for others. I wish I could say that wasn't true of me too. I have hung out with my friend, "denial," for long periods of time. People can be good and clueless at the same time. Thankfully, since my family's secret past came to light, I have become sensitized to the terrible injustices that still play out before us in the theater of racism. Tears and anger, helplessness, guilt, shame, impotence and outrage, visit me and I will not refuse them entry into my heart. I would not wish to go back to the version of blissful abandon that I could slip into before 2006, despite the increasing frequency and visual access to national incidents of racial violence that produce unrelenting grief.

Every time the family of a murdered black person stands before the national media and asks his or her community not to respond in violence, I am ashamed. Every time I see the dignity with which so many black people face the harsh realities of their world, I am humbled and I know that their strength is enviable, though tragic. Every time a black person subdues anger rather than act out against the systems that limit them, I fear that anger may one day erupt and destroy me, and I will deserve it and there will be nothing I can say or do. I see the nobility in black men and women, and I know that it takes lifetimes of pain and suffering to grow into that place of restraint. I want to be part of a society whose white members are able to stare the history of slavery and injustice in the face and en mass and in unison, say, please for the sake of our souls, forgive us and allow us to make things right.

I know that American black people have an intricate, complex and refined way of sourcing themselves for the hard lives they live. Many of them will be okay with me and perhaps even come close to being friends, but I don't expect them to willingly share the beauty and richness of their private interiors. That they bridle their trust is only fair.

Yet, the price of caring holds promise alongside the pain. For me, the journey through darkness has had the surprising effect of opening my heart a little bit more so that I can allow myself to forge connections and appreciate the strength and beauty of people I would not have known before now. When I'm in public and am given a chance to look deeply into the eyes of people unlike me, I am gifted with a smile or a nod or an invitation that I would not otherwise have known.

During vulnerable moments of frustration and despair I reread the words of my friend, Norma, a black poet living in Denver, Colorado. "Molly, don't be so hard on yourself. Your ancestors and mine are helping us even now, as we speak and share these stories. They aren't stagnant in the past.

They are helping us now in this moment. They are helping us to pierce the fragile but resistant shield of ignorance, denial and fear so that some light can get in to illuminate that dark, musty and festering place. You are a healer and a leader and a bringer of light. Allow your luminance to radiate."

May 4, 2016. Ancestors. To understand more fully the significance of ancestry to African Americans, I decided to make a pilgrimage to Charleston. For several months I'd picked up on the fact that after the Mother Emanuel massacre on June 17, 2015, the nation was looking to Charleston to be the model city for a new approach to racism. Isabel Wilkerson, wrote in an opinion piece that the city might become the epicenter of a New Reconstruction. I felt it was important to drop beneath the veneer of tourism so that I could see the underbelly of the city Conde Nast "Traveler" named the Best U.S. City between 2010 and 2014. That Charleston was founded in 1670 makes it one of our oldest American cities.

I consulted guidebooks and talked with friends familiar with the city. I charted out my course with a degree of uncertainty, knowing that with only a few days, I would miss some important landmarks. My goal was to stay wide open and be as present to my surroundings as I could be. Past solo travels had prepared me for a sojourn in unfamiliar territory. My watchwords? Make space for the unexpected, the coincidental, for quantum connections.

No matter how repulsive it is to take in the visual imagery that goes along with slavery, I felt that as a white, middle class American woman, one whose own family was involved in slavery, I was obligated to look at it full on without flinching. One of the first sites I visited was the Old Slave Mart

Museum, dedicated in 2007 by then Charleston Mayor, Joe Riley. The cobbled street in front of the museum originally known as Thomas Ryan's slave mart beckons visitors into the mid 1800s. Imagine the long journey over water from the shores of Africa chained and confined in small spaces, disembarking on the barrier islands off the coast of South Carolina. The cost of an ordinary black man in 1860, for example, was $1100 to $1250, equivalent to $26,000 to $30,000 in 2007. This level of human trafficking made Charleston one of the wealthiest cities in our country.

Walking about the museum, peering at displays of artifacts and photographs, I was reminded of my first visit to the Holocaust Museum in Washington, D.C. Here, in Charleston, the dimly lit, musty atmosphere became increasingly stifling the longer I stayed, and the dark, tragic energy of the place seemed to cover me like a damp blanket. I longed to get outside in the sunshine and to breathe some fresh air. Yet somehow, this place offered me an opportunity to restrain my instincts and experience the gravity of subjugation. It was the first indication I encountered of the city's efforts to own and honor the past.

After I exited the building, I walked east toward the seawall. The sunshine was brilliant that day. Clouds like misshapen cotton balls lazed about in a cobalt blue sky. Cooler than usual for May, the breeze coming in off the ocean almost called for a sweater. Even so, I stopped at a tourist site for an ice cream cone, then meandered over to Waterfront Park where a lovely fountain in the shape of a pineapple threw spray into the air. Off in the distance Fort Sumter stands guard over the Charleston Harbor. I thought about the scene in 1861 when the first shots of the Civil War were fired there. Earlier that day I'd noticed the tourism hawkers on the streets offering guided tours to the harbor, the plantations, the garden district—the French Quarter. I'd walked through the old Exchange building with its guides in period costumes who talked about the pirates once housed in the basement dungeon and of George Washington's visit there. I spent an hour walking through the city market where vendors sold their wares and Gullah Geechie women sat in the shade, weaving their sweet grass baskets. The practice of making these baskets was brought from the Rice Coasts of West Africa. Here, as there, it would be used to extract rice from chaff after the harvest. I looked in the faces of those craftswomen and understood that they were simultaneously making a living off tourists, while keeping an heirloom craft alive, but I didn't see joy. There seemed to be little camaraderie amongst them. Many looked bored and indifferent to tourists. At the end of the day, they had to be tired.

I walked the streets South of Broad where the wealthy, landed gentry whiled away their days in houses built in such a way as to ward off the merciless, humid climate of the seaboard. Waterfront mansions painted in various pastel hues: pink, yellow, blue, please the eye and reflect the hard work of city fathers, whose desire it was and still is to build and now preserve the unique architectural style dominated by columns, gabled roofs, ornate plasterwork and brickwork. Gifted black tradesmen embellished the city's unique décor and made major contributions to the arts with little acknowledgement. They were governed by the Slave Code of 1740, which mandated that it was against the law to teach a slave to read or write, but they could develop manual skills by apprenticing with master craftsmen when not working to cultivate fields of rice and later cotton.

I found my way to Blake Street to the home and work-shop of Phillip Simmons, born in 1912, who became an apprentice to a blacksmith and devoted his life to decorative ironwork that beautifies homes and churches throughout the older sections of the city. Gates, fences, balconies and window grills charm visitors. Simmons died in 2009, ever humble and true to his craft. For many of his gates he fashioned hot iron into the shape of hearts. I couldn't know until later in my trip how that would play into my perceptions of the city. In 1982 the National Endowment for the Arts bestowed on Simmons the prestigious National Heritage Fellowship.

The countryside surrounding the city is dotted with major plantations like Boone
Hall, Magnolia, Middleton Place and Drayton Hall. Early in his tenure in Charleston,
Gregory posted about his own pilgrimage to a rice plantation. I wondered if his experience there weighed heavily on his heart. He doesn't specify which plantation he visited but later in the first day of my Charleston trip, I thought of him as I drove out to James Island to the McLeod Plantation, which I had chosen to visit because of the well preserved slave quarters, the fields where once sea island cotton grew in abundance, and because of its importance in the movement to free slaves. My curiosity was piqued because many of the travel guidebooks I consulted before my trip did not mention it.

Molly Walling

Approaching the McLeod mansion and slave quarters (built in 1854) on foot that spring afternoon, I was swept up in the quiet and the evidence of the industry of the workers who by physical strength and force of will made this plantation exceedingly productive for 150 years. The aura created by immense oak trees flocked in Spanish moss took me back to my family's home and acres of cotton fields in Mississippi. On our farm, work was begun at sunrise and finished at sunset. Here, workers labored under a task system so that when specified jobs were completed, there was the potential for remaining time in the day to be used as one pleased. The community of 83 people that lived and worked at McLeod appeared to have accepted and labored together well under the system, but this was considered a "middle class farm," and it doesn't compare to other more lavish plantations. The tiny, one room, whitewashed cottages stand in stark relief to the grandeur of the Georgian master's house. Each one has a fireplace, but today they remain empty of artifacts, and that worked to my advantage. Walking about the grounds alone, staring into the small open spaces of these houses, I had the experience I came to Charleston for: I felt, right up against my skin, the spirits of those who had lived and died there. I could imagine slaves gathering after a day of hard labor, sitting by the fire, telling stories, singing songs, in exhausted dignity.

McLeod has an interesting history in that during the Civil War it was occupied by black soldiers from Massachusetts. In 1865, the federal government created the Freedman's Bureau to assist newly freed slaves and disenfranchised poor whites. The tenant farming system was instigated. A freed slave was given 40 acres and a mule, though that changed when Andrew Johnson entered office and voided the law. The Bureau lasted until 1869. According to the Census of 1870, the McLeod family was once again in residence and farming continued as South Carolina transitioned into freedom.

At about the time the Freedman's Bureau held residence at McLeod, it was also instrumental in the creation of another important landmark in Charleston, one that few visitors make a part of their sojourn, the Avery Research Center for African American History and Culture, which has been a part of the College of Charleston since 1985. In 1865, the Bureau along with the American Missionary Association and the Avery family provided seed money for the construction of the Avery Normal Institute. A private school, the K-12 institute provided teacher training and educated young black children in classical education. Some of those students went on to become teachers and some, like Septima Poinsette Clark, fought for civil rights. Having been a teacher most of my life I was interested in the fact that during the days of the Avery Institute, the highest pay a black teacher could expect was $675, while the lowest pay for a white teacher was $1100. After desegregation, the building became the repository for many important African American artifacts as well as manuscript collections, photographs, artwork and other records.

Of interest to me was a collection of badges dating back to the 1800s. Unique to Charleston was the practice of licensing slaves for hire outside their owners' purview. The badges did not have names on them but they did have the date and a job category listed. For example, one of the metal tags was stamped with the year 1813, the job—Porter, and the city's name, Charleston. The way this system worked, a slave could be hired out for a period of time but the money he or she was paid was shared with his owner.

As I was the only visitor in the collection that day, I had a private tour with one of the curators, Leah Worthington. She told me the story of Denmark Vesey, who wore a badge similar to others in the museum. Denmark was one of the founders of the Mother Emanuel A.M.E. Church in 1816. Black churches played an important role in the political life of slaves. Denmark won a lottery and with his earnings bought his freedom. He did not have enough money to free his wife and children. As his influence grew, he and others conspired to revolt, slaughter their white bosses and sail to Haiti. Somehow his plans became known to the white estab-lishment and in 1822 Mother Emanuel was burned to the ground. Vesey and twenty-two others were hanged. Then came harsher laws. While Leah told me this story, I couldn't help thinking of Gregory. Since his ancestors came from the Rice Coasts of West Africa, might they have come through Charleston moving west on the slave route: Charleston to Augusta to Atlanta to Montgomery to Jackson to Anguilla? What if Denmark Vesey had been successful in his revolt? How would life in Charleston and throughout the South have been different?

Intimacy of community life in the historic parts of the city was evident. Churches were everywhere, built right into the residential areas and next to places of business. As time passed, some of the black cemeteries became part of the substructure of newer buildings. An effort is ongoing to excavate and retrieve ancient tombstones.

African Americans had social strata of their own. As the races intermingled more and more, there became varying "shades of black." Some of the freed slaves became slave owners. Many fled and made it out of the South. Fifty thousand ran away each year. While ambling through the streets I noticed, on occasion, a sculptured angel inside a fenced yard. A guide told me that those angels were placed on the grounds of the residences of individuals who died in the 2015 massacre at Mother Emanuel.

MY FRIEND VIRGINIA SCHENK IS A JAZZ SINGER WITH connections in the arts community in Charleston. To enhance my vision of the early Africans that landed on the shores of this country, I wanted to meet and talk with someone of Gullah descent. Virginia introduced me to two women who told me their stories and shared the culture of their people. Teena was one of the most beautiful young women I had ever seen. She lived in Atlanta , growing organic food and making her living as a chef. When she came into the kitchen where I was staying, I was immediately caught up in her aura of quiet, soft, glowing self-possession. She wore native African garments in bright and colorful patterns. Her hair was completely hidden, tied up in a cloth and wrapped in a knot the size of a peony in full bloom that rested on one side of her forehead. Her wide, expressive eyes were sometimes downcast as she moved with grace about the kitchen, chopping, slicing and boiling. From her large woven basket she produced fresh herbs that she combined in unique meatless dishes. The food went down with ease and filled my mouth with delightful textures and flavors.

When we could draw Teena out of the kitchen, she told us that for generations her ancestors were enslaved farmers and fishermen that had lived on Amelia Island, one of the southernmost barrier islands, or Sea Islands, considered Gullah. She said, "They lived on and near the land long before the green movement." She emphasized the importance of ancestors and their strong presence in her life. This was a woman whose essential nature was what she presented to the world. More important than what she said or what she had done in her life was the pure expression of her inner being. I had the clear sense that I could learn much more from her. She intimated familiarity with the occult aspect of her culture. A cursory look at the history of the Gullah indicates a strong intention on the part of enslaved Africans to preserve their original language, rituals, folk wisdom and food ways. Illnesses like malaria and yellow fever plagued the islanders so they relied heavily on herbal medicine, roots, bark and tea. They had remedies for spiritual and social ills as well. They used amulets and talismen to ward off the deeds of evil spirits. Gullahs also believed in the "undead" and spirit guides that watch over and protect them. This arcane aspect of the Gullah culture breathed its way into the larger societies of Charleston and Savannah. I first became interested when I read John Berendt's book, *Midnight in the Garden of Good and Evil* .

Late in the afternoon of my last day on the coast, another visitor rapped on the door of the beach house. Ann Caldwell, well-known in Charleston for her fabulous alto-contralto voice, performs jazz, Negro spirituals, pop and chamber music. She and the Magnolia Singers hold regular gatherings with congregations in the city to perform in the circular style of the praise house. Still extant in coastal areas are these small churches built on plantations during the days of slavery.

For the following two hours, Ann told her story of growing up Gullah in Denmark, South Carolina. She paused only to garnish her narrative with song. It didn't take long for me to appreciate how fortunate I was to be in the presence of this extraordinary woman and to remember with fondness the rich black musical heritage that I had experienced as a young woman in Mississippi. According to Ann, the rhythms of spirituals came from Africa. Field workers would often sing while they worked. The tempo set the pace of their labor. In churches and in their homes, they could describe moments, situations, surroundings, feelings, through song. As an expressive outlet, songs were a natural way to cope with oppression, poverty, disrespect and violence. Ann said, "People sang because they had to. In those days there were no drugs for depression or hopelessness. There was no Prozac. They sang themselves happy." They sang themselves happy....

Today there are over 6,000 documented spirituals. When performed in Praise Houses, they witness to a particular history while evoking the spirits of ancestors. "Guide my feet while I run this race for I don't want to run this race in vain" expresses a common core belief that there will be redemption in the next life, if only the people can survive the hardship they face. Often choristers utilized a form called "Ring Shout." They stood in a circle to sing, so as to gather a sense of unity and wholeness. In this ritual, movement was counterclockwise. Participants not only sang together but they shuffled, stomped their feet, and clapped their hands. For them, the practice was a way of affirming that the physical body mattered, that joining others who knew and understood the hardships of life in the South would help them to triumph over their oppressors. Many of the spirituals addressed the Lord directly.

White southerners were seriously intent on "Christianizing" the slaves. Introduction to the Bible and to the message of Christ seeped into the religious practice of the Gullah. In some instances they reinterpreted it to fit their circumstances.

Ann explained that the lyrics they sang often contained coded messages for those who wanted to escape. For example, the word "Canaan" referred to Canada; "chariot" referred to the railroad train. Most southerners are familiar with "Wade in the Water." This song was sung to warn runaways that dogs were on their trail, and to seek safety in the water. To encourage and give directions, the songs became exceedingly important. "Follow the drinking gourd" indicated that the Big Dipper was a way to navigate to safety.

As Ann gifted us with story and song, I was reminded once again that people of color have much to teach me about community, about grace, about heart. The intrinsic values of their culture can best be discovered in relationships in which both parties are on equal footing. We have denied the world by failing to keep their stories alive. It's time to go to the praise house and sing together.

> Call: *This little light of mine*
> Response: *I'm gonna let it shine*
> Call: *This little light of mine*
> Response: *I'm gonna let it shine*
> Call: *This little light of mine*
> Response: *I'm gonna let it shine*
> All: *Let it shine, let it shine, let it shine.*

Now, years after the shootings at Mother Emanuel, the city of Charleston, known for being courteous and gracious, has begun to return to normal, to the established routines that have been in place for years. The outpourings of kindness and unity that followed the massacre and other racial nightmares may have become less visible but this city has come a long way since the Unity Movement began with a march on the Ravenel Bridge. Clearly Charlestonians have engaged in deep reflection, open discussion and decisive action to take responsibility for positive change. For example, I read that the police force has embraced a more transparent approach to law enforcement. Officers seek out opportunities to connect with at-risk communities. There is a new level of trust built into relationships, but change is just beginning. For it to last, young men and women of color, we hope, will be willing to relinquish their fear and aggression so that trust can be maintained on both sides.

I wanted to get a feel for the state of systemic inequality in Charleston and found an interview in "Charlie" magazine featuring a South Carolina State Senator. From his perspective as a black legislator representing parts of Charleston and Dorchester Counties, he is committed to continuing and deepening the city's focus on three areas: the education system, healthcare, and economic disparity. He believes that every child, regardless of socio-economic background, should have a quality education. "The greatest resource a state has is an intelligent and healthy citizenry/workforce." The problems associated with racism hinge on better economic opportunities for people of color. For Charleston to rebrand itself, it will take the hard work of many people. There is hope. Black lives are starting to matter more in Charleston.

2018

The Charleston City council passed a resolution that set out an official apology for slavery 155 years after. It was passed by a 7-5 vote.

Early 2020

The International African American Museum will open to the public—113 Calhoun Street—site of the Gadsden Wharf where 40% of all American slaves disembarked.

Chapter 17

TINY VILLAGES
EVERYWHERE

———⊗∞⊘———

June 2016. Four years after meeting the descendants of Simon Toombs, it was time to catch up, so I called Pat to check on Virginia. Little had changed at 130th Street, Compton. Virginia was living out her days confined to a hospital bed, totally dependent on Pat. To provide this level of care day in and day out would seem to make even the most patient person feel anchored in place if not trapped. That Pat supported her like this without complaint was inspiring. She worked hard to provide nutritious meals, but Virginia was losing weight anyway.

"I try to keep her eating. She's not sickly or nothing other than her condition and she has a good attitude. She's alert and in a happy place. She's less combative but she tries to charm me into doing things for her."

"Who taught you how to be a caregiver?" I asked.

"Mama Lilly."

Charlie Lee Sr., Pat's grandfather, married his second wife, Lilly, and brought her to California with him. She stepped in to watch out for Virginia's three children when they were left unattended by an inebriated mother. Mama

Lilly was a giver, and Pat came to regard her as an angel. "She would give anything to anyone to make their life better—even people she didn't know. If she had three dollars and someone was hungry, she'd make a pot of soup and stretch it out." Pat believes that she learned survival skills from Mama Lilly too. At one point in Pat's life, Mama Lilly offered to give her money to buy a house, but Pat refused it. She felt unready to assume that kind of responsibility and shied away from taking Mama Lilly's money, but she did soak up her love and advice. She told her granddaughter, "Patsy, don't ever put a fella down when he down. That ain't right."

As a child, Pat eavesdropped on the adults gathered together. Charlie Lee, Mama Lilly and Aunt Mat, after her move to L.A., talked about the Mississippi they had known. She'd heard her mother cry about her father's death, but it was through storytelling that Pat learned more details and subsequently passed them along to Latoya. A counterpoint to the tragedy of losing Simon was the regard Aunt Mat had for my grandmother. I smiled when Pat said, "She would say how good your grandmother was to her—she said they were good friends."

On the day I called Pat, she was coping with the destruction caused by a freak "mini-tornado" that touched down in Compton. It reduced part of the cement wall around her property to rubble. Five months after the "disaster", workmen were starting to repair the damage that would not have happened if Charlie Lee had put rebar in the original structure when he built the house. Pat said, "My neighbors are good. They've got chicken coops. That's what I'm upset about. Right now the chickens don't come over here. The ducks don't come over here, but their dog does bother me." She would not admit to feeling vulnerable but I couldn't help thinking that she was spending more time around her home and riding her bike less often because she didn't feel comfortable leaving Virginia alone. I wondered what Pat's life would be like when she no longer had her mother to care for, when she was alone. One thing is clear, Pat is resilient.

When I asked if she could pinpoint the one thing she would change about her life, her response was revealing. "During the 1970s, when I was in my 20s, I decided I wanted to get into commercials. I went down to Hollywood to a place on Cherokee Street, and they told me I needed a portfolio. It cost $200 and some so I paid." In the meantime, she told Charlie Lee, her dad, what she was doing. He said, "You gotta watch those people. All they want to do is take your money. You're not going anywhere. They're gonna want more money."

When Pat went for her photo shoot, she was positioned in a cubicle next to a tall, handsome black man. "I took good pictures. They came out pretty good and I still have the portfolio." But Dad kept saying don't be giving up your money. I believed him. I was stupid, and I regret that I listened to my dad and I didn't follow through on my own instincts." Six months later, she discovered that the good looking man posing next to her was Clarence Williams III. He got a role on Mod Squad and became the iconic actor who sported a large frizzy afro for his part as the hippie cop, Linc. Pat has to wonder from time to time about where she would be now if she had pursued that dream. Would she have taken on roles that were later played by actresses like Alfre Woodard, Phylicia Rashad, Angela Bassett?

"I was a footloose happy person then. I didn't let any-thing get me down so I moved on, but I used to act around the house, imitating people ... a rich southerner, someone

I heard on TV... I acted and had everybody laughing. It just came out natural."

During the course of our conversation, Pat slipped into mime from time to time, so I can attest to her talent. She had me laughing too. She would be great at acting in community theater productions.

Facebook post dated June 22, 2015 (5 days after the shooting at Mother Emanuel).

Latoya Mills Dennis:
One of my take-aways from church yesterday is that in two months all will be forgotten in SC, and we as a people will be on to the next tragedy. I've always said it's not enough to just take care of your household. We have to get our hands dirty...heck...Our whole body dirty and demand more for our children....biological/non biological...even the ones who are easy to throw away to the world. Your kids are exposed to the views and opinions of other people's children. If we don't start seeing all these kids as a responsibility, the problems within our communities will keep us stagnant.

When I first met Latoya at Pat's house in 2012, her demeanor and presence were arresting. She had a quiet dignity about her, and when she told me about winning a seventh grade competition with her dramatic monologue about Simon's death, I saw the first signs of social activism in her. Under the surface was a persona comfortable speaking in public.

The motivation that led her down a long and determined path started over twenty years ago when she worked for a California drug rehab program that took women directly from the court system, many of whom were pregnant or had small children. In the 90s, during the height of the crack era, she transitioned to half-way houses where she supported women who were leaving corrections after a term of incarceration. She helped them to reconnect with family, find jobs, get an ID and prepare to reintegrate into society.

The work helped her to mature and realize that she was a good mentor. Recently she found some letters from when she was in junior high and high school. Proudly she recalled the contents. "You are such a comfortable person to talk to." "Thank you for listening." "Thank you for the advice."

Once Latoya became aware of the ease with which she could speak in public, she wanted to sharpen her communication skills, find some new tools and learn all she could. "I knew I wanted to be a better speaker. I knew that somehow what I was being led to do would involve public speaking and I was already comfortable in front of an audience." When an invitation arrived from the local chapter of Toastmasters, Latoya saw an opportunity to obtain the training she needed. Begun in 1924 at the YMCA in Santa Ana, California, Toastmasters has grown to an international organization with chapters in 135 countries. Once again, the valuable role of mentoring came into play only this time she, herself, was the recipient of coaching.

At the Toastmasters meetings, Latoya found a kindred spirit, Kama, who had started a non-profit for victims of domestic violence. Every two weeks the two met to share ideas and support each other's dreams. Latoya benefited from watching her friend put together an event. She was inspired and motivated. "I thought...I'm already having conversations with girls in a very respectful way, not crossing the line and talking about things that they need to talk about with their moms." Latoya branded her future nonprofit "Gyrl Talk" and on June 13, 2015, she held her first workshop with two presenters who were experts on domestic violence and sex trafficking. Thirty two mothers and daughters attended. Latoya envisioned small group discussions. She was very clear about the importance of the mother/daughter relationship and hoped to encourage deeper bonding.

When I spoke with Latoya, I wasn't fully aware of the persistent and insidious problems associated with human trafficking. That this trade was a step-child of the slavery evident in the history of the south made perfect sense, but when I began to research, I discovered how widespread this crime has become. In an article in the January 28, 2016 *L.A. Times*, Veronica Rocha reported on a two day investigation that resulted in the arrest of 198 people in Los Angeles County. "Six women and 12 minors, mostly African American, were identified as trafficking victims who had been used for sexual slavery."

Traffickers work under the radar of public scrutiny by silencing their victims, by making them feel complicit in the sexual behavior they are forced to carry out. The *Atlantic Magazine* published "Sex Trafficking Goes Unnoticed in America," by Priscilla Alvarez, in February 2016. "Traffickers also play into the narrative by telling victims, who are exploited for sex, that they are offenders, threatening to call the police and report them for prostitution if they push back." Victims who are drawn into commercial sex by gangs or pimps are often young teens who have become vulnerable due to insufficient parental involvement. What Latoya aspired to do with Gyrl Talk was to help provide young women with the tools they need to make good decisions in pressured situations.

I asked her if she was beginning to see positive results from her work. She admitted that her full-time job as an insurance adjuster and workman's comp administrator left only her evenings and weekends to plan events. In the fall of 2015, the Greater Faith Ministries Church booked Latoya's event, whose theme was "Body Image: My Body My Temple." Soon after that she'd been successful in applying for and receiving 501C3 status, but she still experienced frustration from time to time because of the amount of organization required to do two jobs. With inadequate cash flow, she sometimes has to dip into her own earnings to cover the cost of events.

Proof of success has come through a different organization. Latoya was instrumental in starting a girls' club at her daughter's high school. One afternoon a week, she and her Toastmasters friend, Kama, have watched as the meeting place for the club that housed only a few girls at first is now full to overflowing. The meetings offer the girls a safe haven for developing trust and camaraderie so that they open up about the pressures they face. Before the club began there was considerable back-biting and fighting amongst the girls in the high school. Now there is a new dimension to their relationships in the form of sisterhood. Latoya is deeply committed to making sure that the next generation is "better than ours."

Our conversation morphed into one about the state of racial injustice in our country. "One thing I'm most grateful for is all the people whose names we will never know who stood up, who marched, who left their families knowing that they probably wouldn't return, knowing that they were putting a mark on their own families but who stood up for something because they wanted the future to change. This was a future they knew they would never see, but hopefully the generations to come would see." We talked about what our country needs most so that racial healing can begin.

I said, "It's time for us Caucasians to do something symbolic."

"An apology and some kind of commemoration of our ancestors—that would be the start of healing," she responded. "It doesn't take much—a national holiday to acknowledge slavery, Jim Crow, the rest of it. Most of us are so far beyond 40 acres and a mule but how about just an apology—something that reminds us every year that we are beyond that. The feeling is that even though our ancestors built the country, we are still visitors here."

In June 2016, Latoya posted on Facebook that she had become the new president of Toastmasters of Riverside, California.

After high school, Gregory went to Clark Atlanta University, an historically black college. The major benefits of his college experience commenced when he spent a year in the Dominican Republic, where he developed a deep and nurturing relationship with his host family, became bi-lingual, and later, met a Dominican woman, Massiel Calderon.

"I can't explain to you how we got together. I met her at a Christian camp, but I wasn't pursuing her and she wasn't pursuing me." Massiel is beautiful, and when her picture appeared on Facebook, he wondered who that "random" girl could be. They started communicating via social media and the superficial relationship they started out with didn't develop until she traveled to Maryland for a summer exchange program focused on English as a second language. Soon she was visiting Gregory in Charleston while he was reporting on the violent racial events that were opening the nation's eyes to a reality no one wanted to acknowledge. According to Latoya, "It was energy draining—too much emotion for him to take in at once. To have to be right there talking to the family of people who died at Mother Emanuel, didn't leave him. He had a hard time moving on to the next event." For that reason, Massiel provided a needed counterbalance to the extremes of Gregory's life.

When he decided to leave the South and go home, Massiel drove across country with him. He introduced her to his family and friends, took her to his church. She blended in well in every situation. For him, her best quality is patience. "It wasn't a quality that she had. My mind goes a million miles an hour. My body goes two million miles an hour." She's okay with that. She's okay with his emotionality, with his drive. Gregory says he is stable for the first time since he left home for college nearly ten years ago. He's reconnected with his extensive family, settled into an apartment in Fresno, and now he's partnering with this young woman who has dreams and ambition of her own, who has stayed by his side.

Gregory and Massiel became engaged on January 7, 2017. With his help, she is going through the immigration process. He has had clear boundaries that dictate the course of their involvement. Massiel has managed to find a program that will pay for her to come to the states and fund the training she needs to get credentialed as a teacher. She will have to commit to two years in an elementary school position but Gregory sees her moving on from there. Due to his student loans, he would not propose to her until she secured her stateside job. He listened to Pat's advice when she told him early on that he wouldn't be happy if he didn't know where his next dollar would come from.

At that time, Gregory was satisfied with his work. When I asked him to describe the issues he reported on he said, "It's totally different from Charleston. There it was all about black and white, all about police and race relations. Here it's all about immigration and the Hispanic push for reform so that they can become legalized citizens. I've learned that Fresno is the top farming area in the country and possibly the world. If we didn't have Hispanics, who would be out there working those fields?" Fortunate for the farmers, Gregory is speaking their language and keeping them informed about their status in the States.

When I asked Gregory what else he wants to accomplish in his life, he was quiet for a long moment before answering. "I'm still a work in progress, but I know that what I want, money can't buy. Look at the celebrities. They're stressed out. They're dying. Michael Jackson died. Prince died. Whitney Houston died. I've noticed though that whether people have a million dollars or one dollar, they are stressed out. I just hope I get to that place spiritually where I'm financially happy and emotionally happy, where I can have peace and joy, where I know I did the right thing and found balance in my life."

WOULD SIMON BE PROUD OF HIS GREAT-GREAT-grandson? We do know that in his last hours, Simon wore his pride in his army jacket. Service to his country in a world war had heightened his sense of self-worth. He was unprepared and unwilling to have anyone take it from him, so he refused to back down in the face of great peril. I believe that Simon would feel that Gregory has much to be proud of.

A desire to know about his family led him to read *Death in the Delta* and to reach out to me. It was his destiny to work in Charleston, and he stepped up to do the job, determined to capture the news in an unbiased and accurate way. Once there, his desire to know about the lives of his ancestors led him to Middleton Place, a prominent plantation home. He told me, "I didn't go there for my job. I went there to learn about myself." Maybe it was important to him to test his own response to the limitations of a life in slavery, so that he would know how important it was to Simon to stand against it. His tenure in Charleston brought him as close to Simon's final hour as he could get. He knows the ugly face of racial violence close up, and in time his sensitivity to the suffering of others motivated him to leave the South and go back to a more tolerant part of the country where he could pursue his career in journalism. It is too early to determine the gifts of the hard, eye-opening experience of Charleston in 2015, but Gregory has learned the importance of balance, family, faith, and love. And White America is waking up to systemic racism, it is essential and empowering that men and women such as Gregory are working to make sure we cannot forget, cover up, or deny what happened in our own personal past, and in the past of our nation.

Chapter 18

HAWKS

I'M SITTING IN MY SUNROOM ON A SUNNY, CLEAR DAY in August 2016.

My view outside the picture window draws me to this spot every morning. Mountains dressed in a mix of hues of green are sometimes awash in mist, sometimes hidden behind dense rain clouds, sometimes in full regalia. Today, way off in the distance, a hawk soars above the steepest elevation, riding the currents. He appears to be surveying the forest below, utilizing every part of his body in perfect harmony with the wind. With the slightest tilt of his wings he circles around to some new vista. He is one of a whole society of hawks. Like all of the others, his tenure here on earth will be unremarkable, yet his presence offers us a vision of grace, trust, confidence.

For Simon is a book about a flock of people, just ordinary people, whose lives would not have connected except for one predatory act that resulted in premature, unwarranted death. Simon's family trusted me enough to share their history with me. Because they so graciously took me into their home and into the tiny room where Simon's daughter, Virginia, lives, they gave me a precious opportunity. From his portrait that hangs on the wall beside Virginia's bed, Simon observed our gathering. The lift of his shoulders and chest, the press of his green army jacket, the dignity and pride in his face, created in me a sense that he was right there with us in spirit. To his daughter I said how sorry I was for the actions of my father and his brothers. In that moment, I started to care deeply about this family, these extraordinary, ordinary people—like me—like most of us. I understood, in that moment, that I had personal work to do. My process of discovery required me to investigate my heritage, my privilege and my responsibility to love all people. My research and study have been imperfect, disjointed and incomplete but necessary and I hope sufficient.

Now, I think of Virginia, Pat, Latoya, and Gregory as family. Though we are separated by more than two thousand miles, I have no doubt that our connection is sacred.

November 2018. Virginia Anderson died peacefully. Following is the tribute written for her by great-great grandson, Gregory Woods.

In Loving Memory of Virginia B. Anderson
November 04, 1932 – October 25, 2018

McCormick Mortuary
635 S. Prairie Ave Inglewood, CA 90301
November 12, 2018 1:00pm

Virginia B. Anderson was born to Simon Toombs and Beatrice Farrar on Nov. 4, 1932 in Anguilla, Mississippi. Virginia was primarily raised by her grandmother Leana while her father served five years in the U.S. Army and fought in World War II. As a child, Virginia developed a love for reading and found more enjoyment from literature than playing outside. The depth of Virginia's intellect provided her the opportunity to attend school at a time when most black children picked cotton. This privilege opened up a new world of learning, where she excelled. At 15 years old, Virginia married her love, Charlie Anderson II, and the two headed to Los Angeles.

During their union Charles Anderson III, Patricia Haynes, Simon

Bernard Anderson and Arthur "Van" Anderson were born. Charlie and Virginia eventually divorced. She later gave birth to two more children: Gwendolyn McLeod and Robert "Tiny" Bush. In 1958, Virginia moved to the Aliso Village Housing Projects in East Los Angeles where she quickly gained a reputation for her homemade southern dishes, and desserts made from scratch. People came from all around the city just to catch a bite of her delicious food. Virginia continued to nurture her love of learning by enrolling into Los Angeles City College to earn her associate degree. Although she was a student, Virginia was often asked by her instructors to assist in teaching and grading papers. Her talents extended into the music world, where she wrote songs for various recording artists—most notably Johnny Mathis.

Virginia lived her later years in Compton with her daughter Patricia, who tirelessly cared for her. During that time, her children, grandchildren, great-grandchildren and great-great-grandchildren continuously surrounded her with love and support. Virginia will always be the lady in the front house who greeted everyone with a smile, shared her humorous spirit and was always down to toast a drink with you. Her bubbly energetic soul and warm smile will be remembered by all who encountered her.

Virginia is survived by her children and their spouses: Patricia Anderson; Arthur "Van" Anderson; Gwendolyn and Mike McLeod; Robert "Tiny" and Sandy Bush. She is also survived by her sister and brother-in-law, Bobbie and Mike Morris, as well as a host of grandchildren, great-grandchildren, great-great-grandchildren, nieces, nephews, family members and friends. Virginia was beloved by all who knew her.

BIBLIOGRAPHY

Alexander, Michelle. *The New Jim Crow.* New York: The New Press, 2012.

Alvarez, Priscilla, "When Sex Trafficking Goes Unnoticed in America," *Atlantic Magazine.* February 23, 2014. https://www.theatlantic.com/magazine/archive/2014/06/the-case-for-reparations/361631/

Barry, John M. *Rising Tide: The Great Mississippi Flood of 1927.* New York: Simon and Schuster, 1998.

Bennett, Jessica, "How Compton Got Its Groove Back," *Newsweek,* March 23, 2009. https://www.newsweek.com/how-compton-got-its-groove-back-76361

Blau, Max, "Still a Racist Nation: American Bigotry in Full Display at KKK Rally in South Carolina," *Guardian,* July 19, 2015. https://www.theguardian.com/us-news/2015/jul/19/kkk-clashes-south-carolina-racism

Clark-Lewis, Elizabeth. *Living In, Living Out: African American Domestics and the Great Migration.* Washington: Smithsonian Institution Press, 1994.

Coates, Ta-Nehisi, "The Case for Reparations," *Atlantic Magazine,* June 2014. https://www.theatlantic.com/magazine/archive/2014/06/the-case-for-reparations/361631/

Cobb, James C. *The Most Southern Place on Earth*. New York: Oxford University Press, 1992.

Douglas, Kelly Brown, "Why the Black Church Forgives Dylann Roof," *Nation*, July 2, 2015. https://www.the-nation.com/article/archive/why-the-black-church-forgives-dylann-roof/

Frazier, E. Franklin. *The Negro Family in the United States*. Chicago: University of Chicago Press, 1939.

Hicks, Brian, "Slavery in Charleston: A Chronology of Human Bondage in the Holy City," *Charleston Post & Courier*, April 10, 2011. https://www.postandcou-rier.com/news/special_reports/slavery-in-charleston-a-chronicle-of-human-bondage-in-the-holy-city/article_54334e04-4834-50b7-990b-f81fa3c2804a.html

Hughes, Lyn. *An Anthology of Respect*. USA, 2009.

Kennedy, Randall, "Lifting as We Climb," Harper's Magazine, October 2015. https://harpers.org/archive/2015/10/lifting-as-we-climb/

Litwick, Leon F. *Trouble in Mind*. New York: Alfred A. Knopf, 2013.

Remnick, David, "Charleston and the Age of Obama," *New Yorker* , June 2015. https://www.newyorker.com/news/daily-comment-charleston-and-the-age-of-obama.

Rocha, Veronica, "Six Women and 12 Minors," *L.A. Times*, January 28, 2016. https://www.latimes.com/local/lanow/la-me-ln-human-trafficking-operation-20160128-story.html

Suddreth, Charletta, David W. Jackson III, and Katherine Wormer. *The Maid Narratives: Black Domestics in the Jim Crow South.* Baton Rouge: Louisiana State University, 2012.

Ward, Jesmyn. *Men We Reaped.* New York: Bloomsbury, 2013.

Wilkerson, Isabel, "Our Racial Moment of Truth," *New York Times*, July 18, 2015. https://www.nytimes.com/2015/07/19/opinion/sunday/our-racial-moment-of-truth.html

Wilkerson, Isabel. *The Warmth of Other Suns.* New York: Vintage Books, 2010.

Williamson, Marianne, "Race and Repentance in America, *Huffington Post,* January 26, 2015. https://marianne.com/race-and-repentance-in-america/

ACKNOWLEDGMENTS

For Simon: A Journey into Truth and Reconciliation is a reported memoir that flowered into full expression over the course of eight years following the publication of *Death in the Delta: Uncovering a Mississippi Family Secret*. That its printing is soon to become a reality is something of a miracle. There is no way to adequately express my gratitude for the advice, help and encouragement of many people.

Every writer needs a trusted support. For me, I found the encouragement and ready attention of my brother, Jay Fields, to be invaluable. A very fine writer, poet, artist and photographer, Jay kept me on track and contributed to the text in wonderful ways.

Let me also shine a light on Diana Hume George, whom I met while working on an MFA in Creative Nonfiction at Goucher College, 2005. By no small measure of grace, I was attentive enough to see in her the gifts of a truly remarkable editor. Over time I came to think of her as my writing doula. Her consistent dedication to this project and the one before it brought about a fifteen year friendship and working relationship. Her gifts to me cannot be quantified, but they made it possible for my life work to continue even when hope faded.

Over the years many others stepped out of the shadows

to offer guidance. Anna Morgan, former headmistress of Sullins Academy, was my first reader. I want to acknowledge the following people as well: Bruce Kennedy, Dr. Harold Hedges, the poet, Norma Johnson, Virginia Schenck, jazz vocal artist, and loyal friends —Norma Grvich, Glenda Henderson, Miles Mennell, Susan Stewart, Candy Worrell, Lynn Kessler and Lean Carroll.

The Rev. Charlotte Cleghorn, my spiritual director and Laura Mahr, therapist, worked no small measure of magic on my heart and mind. I am indebted to both of them.

Finally, I attribute this writing to my faith. Without it, I would have lost hope, lost patience and failed to trust the signs and wonders that I experienced along the way.

The following verses from T.S. Eliot's "The Journey of the Magi," express my sentiments so well:

*...were we led all that way for
Birth or Death? There was a Birth, certainly,
We had evidence and no doubt. I had seen birth and death,
But had thought they were different; this Birth was
Hard and bitter agony for us, like Death, our death.
We returned to our places, these Kingdoms,
But no longer at ease here, in the old dispensation,
With an alien people clutching their gods.
I should be glad of another death.*

Made in the USA
Columbia, SC
29 July 2020